# THE CAVAQUINHO CHORD BIBLE

## (DGBD Standard Tuning)

by

## Tobe A. Richards

A Fretted Friends Publication for Cabot Books

Published by:
**Cabot Books**
Copyright © 2008 and 2016 by Cabot Books
All rights reserved.

*First Edition February 2008*
*Second Edition February 2016*

ISBN-13: 978-1-906207-39-7

Cabot Books
3 Kenton Mews
Henleaze
Bristol
BS9 4LT
United Kingdom

Visit our online site at www.frettedfriendsmusic.com
*e-mail: cabotbooks@blueyonder.co.uk*

# TABLE OF CONTENTS

# INTRODUCTION

**The Cavaquinho Chord Bible** provides the musician with 1,728 chords in all keys, featuring 68 different chord types, with 3 variations of each standard chord. 144 major slash chords are also included, together with 48 moveable chord shape diagrams (providing access to a further 576 barré and standard moveable chords) making this the most comprehensive reference guide for the cavaquinho currently available. For many years now, guitarists have been able to pick up a songbook and instantly play the songs in front of them, either with the help of one of the many published guides, or through the chord boxes supplied with most popular music. With the help of this *Chord Bible*, beginners and experienced cavaquinho players alike will be able to take advantage of the many songbooks, fake books and musical compendiums by any artist you would care to name, from *The Beatles* to *Joan Baez*, from *Planxty* to *The Pogues* or *Springsteen* to *Simon & Garfunkel*. With 68 different chordal variations in all keys, virtually any song should be playable!

Having a good chordal knowledge should arguably be the bedrock in any fretted or keyboard musicians armoury. Whether you're playing rock, pop, folk, jazz, blues, country or other types of music, it's impossible to supply a suitable accompaniment to any vocal or solo instrumental music without providing a chordal or harmonic backing. The subtle nuance of an added ninth chord over a major chord is something that can't be captured simply by playing a melody line. In theory it is possible to approximate the harmonic intervals of any music using a limited palette of chords - probably around ten to twelve. But wherever possible it's best to use correct harmonies if they're available to you.

Having four strings, the cavaquinho is obviously limited to four note chords, but by making acceptable compromises and omitting the least important parts of that chord, even the most complex musical structures are possible. For instance, in the case of an eleventh, the third is generally omitted without the character of the chord being adversely affected. Equally, the root or key note isn't always necessary to achieve an effective approximation of the full chord. The third is rarely missing from the majority of chords (other than elevenths) as it determines whether the key is major or minor - although this isn't a hard and fast rule, particularly in folk music where the root and fifth form the basis of most traditional music. These two intervals are generally the starting point for a number of open tunings of instruments as diverse as the guitar, the Irish bouzouki and the mountain dulcimer. The same interval is also used in a lot of heavy rock where a fifth chord is described as a *power chord*. Even though a power chord is technically neither major nor minor, it's more often used as an alternative for a major chord in most popular music.

One question which often pops up is *how many chords do I need to learn?* The smart answer is *'how long is a piece of string?'*, which is true, but it doesn't actually answer the question if you don't know where to start. My advice would be to begin with simple chord clusters like the popular G, C, D and Em progression and gradually work in new ones as you advance. If you intend playing within a rock format, it's probably sensible to learn the E, A, B sequence which is the staple of most guitarists and bassists. As a generalisation, jazz probably requires the greatest chordal knowledge of any form of music, so the learning curve will be longer if you're planning to pick up any songbook and instantly produce a recognisable version of your favourite *Duke Ellington* or *Steely Dan* number. The only truth as far as harmonic knowledge goes is you can never learn *too* much!

In this series of chord theory books, I've included a comprehensive selection of configurations of chords in all keys. As I mentioned previously, this will enable you to pick up virtually any songbook or fake book (topline melody and chord symbols) and look up the chord shape that's needed. Obviously, you'll come across the occasional song which doesn't conform to the normal harmonic intervals which you find in this, or any other chord theory publication, but with a little experimentation and experience, you'll be able to make a reasonable stab at it. For instance, most players would be more than a little bemused if they suddenly came across an instruction to play a *Gbmaj7add6/D*. Fortunately, this is fairly unusual, but from the knowledge you'll have learned, you'll be able to use a similar chord or work it out note by note. Put simply, if every theoretically possible chord shape were to be included in this or any other book, the result would resemble something akin to several volumes of the *Yellow Pages*!

## FINGERING

Always a tricky subject and one which seems to generate a lot of discussion and differing opinions as to which method is correct. Personally, I take the view that it's a largely fruitless exercise, as the number of variables involved make a definitive answer unlikely. So what I've decided to do in this book is to choose fingering positions which feel comfortable to me. Some chord shapes will dictate the fingering used, but others will be down to personal preference. If you can practise your two and three finger chords using different fingers, it will make your playing a lot more fluid when you change to another chord shape. But if you develop habits which limit you to one playing position, it isn't the end of the world either, if you can make the transitions seamless.

The only rules, if you could loosely call them that, are:-

a) Don't abandon using your pinky or little finger if you're just beginning to play, as you'll eventually need it for some of the four finger chords which frequently crop up.

b) Try to avoid fretting with the thumb unless you're learning an instrument like the mountain dulcimer which requires a longer stretch. I know a number of players employ it on slimmer necked instruments, but I personally feel it leads to bad habits.

c) Keep your left hand fingernails short or fretting becomes a major problem. Obviously do the reverse if you're a lefty.

d) If you're a beginner and you're naturally left handed, don't get persuaded into buying a right handed instrument - it won't work! The learning curve will be steeper and you'll never get the fluidity you'd achieve with your natural hand. Most acoustic instruments can be adapted for a left hander apart from cutaway guitars and f-style mandolins etc., by reversing the nut and strings. For the non-reversible instruments, always go for a left handed model.

e) Learn to barré with other fingers apart from your index finger. This will prove invaluable with more complex chords and increase finger strength as well.

f) Don't be afraid to use fingerings further up the neck in combination with open strings as these will give you interesting new voicings and are generally quite popular in folk music. A number of these are provided in this book.

g) The cavaquinho is generally strummed and picked with the fingers. Alternatively, picks or fingerpicks can be used if you're accustomed to this method of playing. Using a pick or fingerpicks generally produces a brighter sound with more attack.

# CHORD THEORY & FAQs

**Q** *What is a chord?*

**A** It's a collection of three or more notes played simultaneously. The exceptions in this book are the fourths and fifths (power chords) which aren't in the strictest sense, true chords. For convenience sake, they are classed as such.

**Q** *What is a triad?*

**A** A chord containing three notes. For example, G Major, Bm, D+ or Asus4.

**Q** *What are intervals?*

**A** Intervals are the musical distance between notes in a musical scale. For instance in the scale of C Major, C is the 1st note, D is the 2nd note, E the 3rd and so on. So if you're playing the chord of C Major, your intervals will be 1–3–5 or C as the *first* note, E as the *third* note and G as the *perfect fifth*.

**Q** *What is a chromatic scale and which intervals does it contain?*

**A:** A chromatic scale encompasses all twelve notes in a musical scale, including the sharps and flats. It's also the basis for the naming of *every* chord in existence. See the staff diagram below to see the intervals:

**Chromatic Scale in C**

Root or 1st · Minor 2nd · Major 2nd · Minor 3rd · Major 3rd · Perfect 4th · Augmented *or* 4th · Diminished 5th · Perfect 5th · Minor 6th · Major 6th · Minor 7th · Major 7th

**Q** *What is a seventh chord?*

**A:** In its most basic form, an additional note beyond the triad. Sevenths can be either major or flattened. For instance, returning to our old friend, the key of C, a *Cmaj7* has an added *B* on top of the *C–E–G* triad. The resultant chord has a mellow quality often found in jazz. Now if you take the B and flatten it by dropping the fourth note in your chord down to a B flat, you get a C7.

**Q:** *Then why isn't it called a C minor seventh?*

**A:** Technically this *is* a minor seventh note, but this would create a lot of confusion when naming chords, as you already have a minor interval option in your triad (in the key of C major, E flat), so it's always referred to as a 7th to differentiate between it and a major seventh.

**Q:** *What is an extension?*

**A:** A chord which goes beyond the scope of triads and sevenths. Basically, extensions are additional notes placed above the triad or seventh in a musical stave, fingerboard or keyboard. It's important to understand these are, for theoretical purposes, always placed above the seventh. Or in layman's terms, higher up the scale. The confusion comes when you start to realise a 9th is identical to a 2nd - in the scale of C – a D note.

**Q:** *So why is the ninth note the same as the second note?*

**A:** This takes a little grasping, but if you remember that if your note goes higher than the seventh it's a 9th, but if it's lower, it'll be a 2nd. An example of this would be Csus2, which contains the root note of C, a 2nd or suspended D note and a G, the perfect 5th. You'll see this even more clearly if you look at the piano keyboard diagram below. Count from the C up to the following D beyond the 7th (B note). From the C to the second D is exactly nine whole notes.

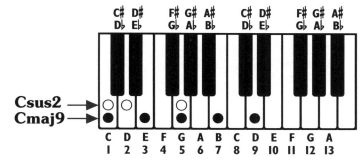

Q: *Do any other extensions share a common note?*
A: Yes, other examples include the *11th,* which is also a *4th* and the *13th* which shares a note with the *6th.*

Q: *What are inversions?*
A: In the root version of a chord, the notes run in their correct order from lowest to highest. In the case of G major, it would be G–B–D. With an inversion of the same chord the notes would run in a different order. For example, the first inversion of G major would be B–D–G and the second, D–G–B. In general, triads sound more or less the same when they're inverted, but that's certainly not the case with sevenths and extensions which can sound quite different and occasionally discordant when the notes are jumbled up in certain configurations. Inversions can also produce different chords using the same basic notes. A good example of this would be *C6 (C-E-G-A)* which produces an *Am7 (A-C-E-G)* when it's inverted (both contain the notes of C–E–G–A, but in a different order). The major variations are in the tonal properties of the chords, making them sound quite different from one another.

Q: *Do elevenths and thirteenths have any particular properties?*
A: Yes. In most cases the 3rd is omitted from eleventh chords and the 11th from the majority of thirteenths as they're deemed unnecessary and arguably, create unwanted dissonance.

Q: *Some chords are called by different names in different music books. What should I do?*
A: The alternative chord name reference chart at the back of the book should help sort out the confusion.

Q: *What is a suspended chord?*
A: It's simpler to think of suspended chords as a stepping stone to a major or resolving chord. In effect the third has been left in a state of suspension by either raising it to a fourth (sus4) or lowering it to a second (sus2). Sevenths also provide versions of the suspended chord in the form of C7sus4 or C7sus2 (using the key of C as an example).

Q: *What is a diminished chord?*
A: A diminished chord has a dissonent quality to it where the third and fifth notes in a triad are flattened by a semi-tone. Again, using C as an example, C major (C-E-G) is altered to Cdim (C-E♭-G♭). A second version of a dimished chord is also used in many forms of music, the diminished seventh. This retains the elements of a standard diminished chord, adding a double flat in the seventh (C-E♭-G♭-B♭♭). A B♭♭ in this case is, to all intents and purposes, really an *A* note.

Q: *What is an augmented chord?*
A: An augmented chord basically performs the opposite task to a diminished one. Instead of lowering the fifth by a semitone, it raises it by the same interval. A C+ (augmented) chord contains the triad of C-E-G♯. The major root and third are retained and the fifth is sharpened.

# UNDERSTANDING THE CHORD BOXES

The three diagrams below show the chord conventions illustrated in this guide. Most experienced fretted instrument players should be familiar with them. The suggested fingering positions are only meant as a general guide and will depend, in many instances, on hand size, finger length and flexibility, so feel free to experiment. The location of the black circles is unalterable, though, if you want to produce the correct voicing.

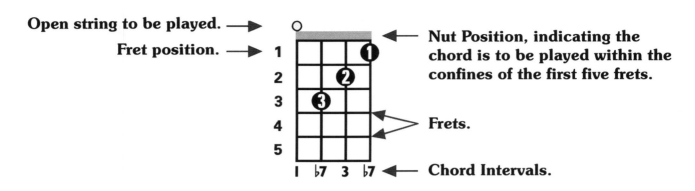

Open string to be played. ➡

Fret position. ➡

Nut Position, indicating the chord is to be played within the confines of the first five frets.

Frets.

Chord Intervals.

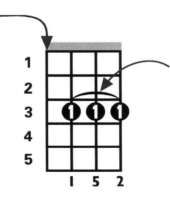

If there are no markers above or below the string, the string should not be played.

Barré chord (in this example, a three string barré to be fretted with the index finger).

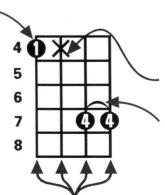

Suggested fingering. In this case the 1st or index finger marker is displayed.

A damped string. In this example the 3rd string should be damped using the lower pad of the middle finger, fretting the 4th string.

A two string barré to be played with the fourth finger.

Left to right: 4th, 3rd, 2nd and 1st courses of strings.

Whether a fretted instrument has single strings or pairs of strings, the chord boxes in this book, other chord dictionaries and songbooks treat it as a four stringed instrument. This convention is common to all double or triple course instruments such as the mandolin or tiple, making the diagrams a lot less confusing and free from unnecessary clutter.

# CAVAQUINHO
# FINGERBOARD & TUNING LAYOUT

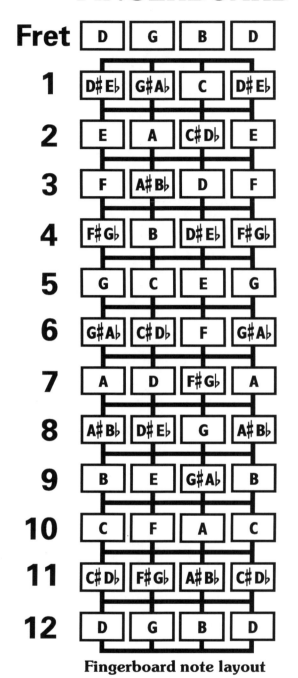

**Fret** D G B D

| | | | | |
|---|---|---|---|---|
| **1** | D#Eb | G#Ab | C | D#Eb |
| **2** | E | A | C#Db | E |
| **3** | F | A#Bb | D | F |
| **4** | F#Gb | B | D#Eb | F#Gb |
| **5** | G | C | E | G |
| **6** | G#Ab | C#Db | F | G#Ab |
| **7** | A | D | F#Gb | A |
| **8** | A#Bb | D#Eb | G | A#Bb |
| **9** | B | E | G#Ab | B |
| **10** | C | F | A | C |
| **11** | C#Db | F#Gb | A#Bb | C#Db |
| **12** | D | G | B | D |

**Fingerboard note layout**

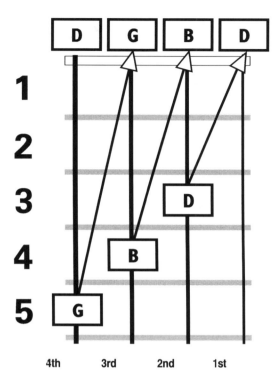

4th 3rd 2nd 1st

**Tuning the cavaquinho by fretting at given intervals on the fingerboard.**

## Notation Tuning Diagram

4th 3rd 2nd 1st

**Cavaquinho DGBD tuning in standard notation.**

To tune your cavaquinho accurately, it's best to use an electronic chromatic tuner, but if there isn't one available, you can tune it to a guitar or piano/electronic keyboard. The following tuning grid gives the correct fingering positions on the guitar fingerboard and piano keyboard.

| Cavaquinho | Guitar | Piano |
|---|---|---|
| 1st string (D) | 1st string (E) fretted at the 10th fret | 2nd D above middle C |
| 2nd string (B) | 1st string (E) fretted at the 7th fret | 1st B above middle C |
| 3rd string (G) | 1st string (E) fretted at the 3rd fret | 1st G above middle C |
| 4th string (D) | 2nd string (B) fretted at the 3rd fret | 1st D above middle C |

# THE CHORDS COVERED IN THIS BOOK

| Chord | Chord Name in Full | Harmonic Interval |
|---|---|---|
| C | Major | 1–3–5 |
| Cm | Minor | 1–F3-5 |
| C-5 | Major Diminished Fifth | 1–3–F5 |
| C° | Diminished | 1–F3—F5 |
| C4 | Fourth | 1–4 |
| C5 | Fifth or Power Chord | 1–5 |
| Csus2 | Suspended Second | 1–2–5 |
| Csus4 | Suspended Fourth | 1–4–5 |
| Csus4add9 | Suspended Fourth Added Ninth | 1–4–5–9 |
| C+ | Augmented | 1–3–S5 |
| C6 | Major Sixth | 1–3–5–6 |
| Cadd9 | Major Added Ninth | 1–3–5–9 |
| Cadd11 | Major Added Eleventh | 1–3–5–11 |
| Cm6 | Minor Sixth | 1–F3–5–6 |
| Cm-6 | Minor Diminished Sixth | 1–F3–5–F6 |
| Cmadd9 | Minor Added Ninth | 1–F3–5–9 |
| C6add9 | Major Sixth Added Ninth | 1–3–5–6–9 |
| Cm6add9 | Minor Sixth Added Ninth | 1–F3–5–6–9 |
| C°7 | Diminished Seventh | 1–F3–F5–DF7 |
| C7 | Seventh | 1–3–5–F7 |
| C7sus2 | Seventh Suspended Second | 1–2–5–F7 |
| C7sus4 | Seventh Suspended Fourth | 1–4–5–F7 |
| C7-5 | Seventh Diminished Fifth | 1–3–F5–F7 |
| C7+5 | Seventh Augmented Fifth | 1–3–S5–F7 |
| C7-9 | Seventh Minor Ninth | 1–3–5–F7–F9 |
| C7+9 | Seventh Augmented Ninth | 1–3–5–F7–S9 |
| C7-5-9 | Seventh Diminished Fifth Minor Ninth | 1–3–F5–F7–F9 |
| C7-5+9 | Seventh Diminished Fifth Augmented Ninth | 1–3–F5–F7–S9 |
| C7+5-9 | Seventh Augmented Fifth Minor Ninth | 1–3–S5–F7–F9 |
| C7+5+9 | Seventh Augmented Fifth Augmented Ninth | 1–3–S5–F7–S9 |
| C7add11 | Seventh Added Eleventh | 1–3–5–F7–11 |
| C7+11 | Seventh Augmented Eleventh | 1–3–5–F7–S11 |
| C7add13 | Seventh Added Thirteenth | 1–3–5–F7–13 |
| Cm7 | Minor Seventh | 1–F3–5–F7 |
| Cm7-5 | Minor Seventh Diminished Fifth | 1–F3–F5–F7 |
| Cm7-5-9 | Minor Seventh Diminished Fifth Minor Ninth | 1–F3–F5–F7–F9 |
| Cm7-9 | Minor Seventh Minor Ninth | 1–F3–5–F7–F9 |
| Cm7add11 | Minor Seventh Added Eleventh | 1–F3–5–F7–11 |
| Cm(maj7) | Minor Major Seventh | 1–F3–5–7 |
| Cmaj7 | Major Seventh | 1–3–5–7 |
| Cmaj7-5 | Major Seventh Diminished Fifth | 1–3–F5–7 |
| Cmaj7+5 | Major Seventh Augmented Fifth | 1–3–S5–7 |
| Cmaj7+11 | Major Seventh Augmented Eleventh | 1–3–5–7–S11 |
| C9 | Ninth | 1–3–5–F7–9 |
| C9sus4 | Ninth Suspended Fourth | 1–4–5–F7–9 |
| C9-5 | Ninth Diminished Fifth | 1–3–F5–F7–9 |
| C9+5 | Ninth Augmented Fifth | 1–3–S5–F7–9 |
| C9+11 | Ninth Augmented Eleventh | 1–3–5–F7–9–S11 |
| Cm9 | Minor Ninth | 1–F3–5–F7–9 |

| Chord | Chord Name in Full | Harmonic Interval |
|---|---|---|
| Cm9-5 | Minor Ninth Diminished Fifth | 1–F3–F5–F7–9 |
| Cm(maj9) | Minor Major Ninth | 1–F3–5–7–9 |
| Cmaj9 | Major Ninth | 1–3–5–7–9 |
| Cmaj9-5 | Major Ninth Diminished Fifth | 1–3–F5–7–9 |
| Cmaj9+5 | Major Ninth Augmented Fifth | 1–3–S5–7–9 |
| Cmaj9add6 | Major Ninth Added Sixth | 1–3–5–6–7–9 |
| Cmaj9+11 | Major Ninth Augmented Eleventh | 1–3–5–7–9–S11 |
| C11 | Eleventh | 1–3–5–F7–9–11 |
| C11-9 | Eleventh Diminished Ninth | 1–3–5–F7–F9–11 |
| Cm11 | Minor Eleventh | 1–F3–5–F7–9–11 |
| Cmaj11 | Major Eleventh | 1–3–5–7–9–11 |
| C13 | Thirteenth | 1–3–5–F7–9–11–13 |
| C13sus4 | Thirteenth Suspended Fourth | 1–4–5–F7–9–11–13 |
| C13-5-9 | Thirteenth Diminished Fifth Minor Ninth | 1–3–F5–F7–F9–11–13 |
| C13-9 | Thirteenth Minor Ninth | 1–3–5–F7–F9–11–13 |
| C13+9 | Thirteenth Augmented Ninth | 1–3–5–F7–S9–11–13 |
| C13+11 | Thirteenth Augmented Eleventh | 1–3–5–F7–9–S11–13 |
| Cm13 | Minor Thirteenth | 1–F3–5–F7–9–11–13 |
| Cmaj13 | Major Thirteenth | 1–3–5–7–9–11–13 |

**Key:   F = Flat     S = Sharp     DF = Double Flat**

# SLASH CHORDS

*What is a slash chord?* Put simply, they're standard chords with an added note in the bass. *So what differentiates a C chord from a C/G when the G is already part of that chord, in this case, the fifth?* Theoretically, nothing, but the difference is very apparent when you actually sound the chord. The G bass is emphasised to provide a different feel to the harmonics. Slashes are also commonly found when the music calls for a descending bassline. For example; C, C/B, C/A and C/G.

**The note after the slash indicates the bass note being played. For instance C/D would be an instruction to play a C chord with a D bass.**

**Slash Note. Generally found on the 4th & 3rd courses.**

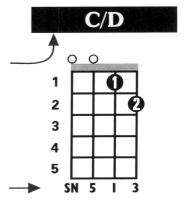

*How do I play a slash chord that isn't listed in this book?* Well, firstly, it would be an almost impossible task to cover every possible slash chord in existence, because the variations are potentially even greater than with standard chords. What you can do, within the confines of this guide, is to find the part of the chord before the slash in the main body of the book and then look for the nearest bass note on the third or fourth course (strings 3 to 4). To find the right bass note, consult the fingerboard layout on *page 9*.

# USING A CAPO (OR *CAPO D'ASTRA*)

Using a capo is a quick and easy way of changing key to suit a different vocal range or to join in with with other musicians playing in a different key. For the uniniated, a capo is a moveable bar that clamps onto the fingerboard of fretted instruments. It works in much the same way as using a finger barré to hold down the strings. They come in a variety of designs and prices, the simplest using a metal rod covered in rubber and sprung with elastic. For the cavaquinho, look for a tenor banjo capo.

# C Chords

| C | Cm | C7 | Cm7 |
|---|----|----|-----|
| 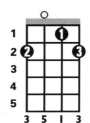 | 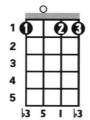 | 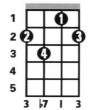 | 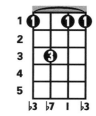 |
| 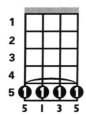 | 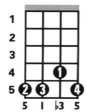 | 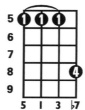 | 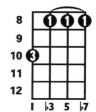 |
| 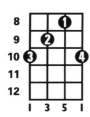 | 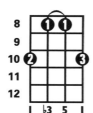 | 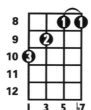 | 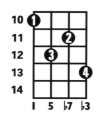 |

| C5 | C6 | Cm6 | Cmaj7 |
|----|----|-----|-------|
| 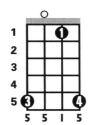 | 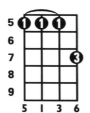 | 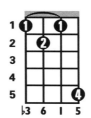 | 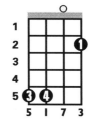 |
| 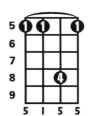 | 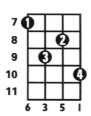 | 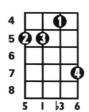 | 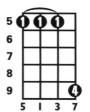 |
| 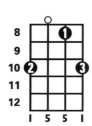 | 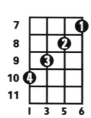 | 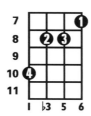 | 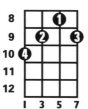 |

## C°
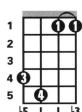
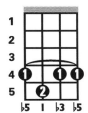
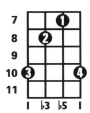

## C°7
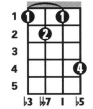
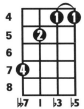
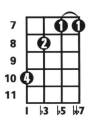

## C-5
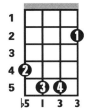
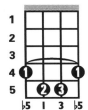
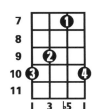

## C+
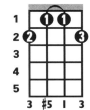
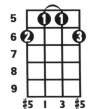
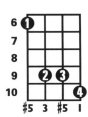

## Csus2
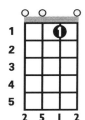
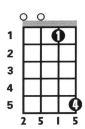
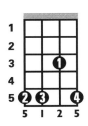

## Csus4
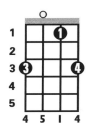
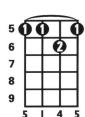
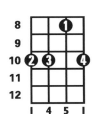

## C7sus4
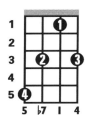
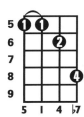
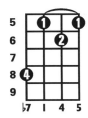

## Cm7-5
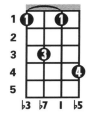
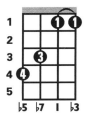
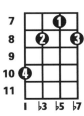

# C Chords

## Cadd9
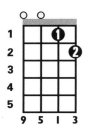
9 5 1 3

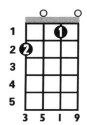
3 5 1 9

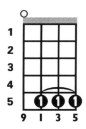
9 1 3 5

## Cmadd9
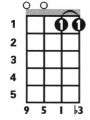
9 5 1 ♭3

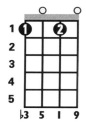
♭3 5 1 9

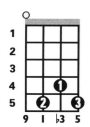
9 1 ♭3 5

## C6add9
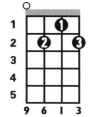
9 6 1 3

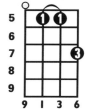
9 1 3 6

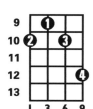
1 3 6 9

## Cm6add9
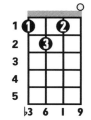
♭3 6 1 9

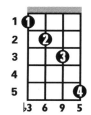
♭3 6 9 5

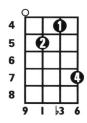
9 1 ♭3 6

## C7-5
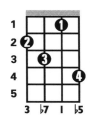
3 ♭7 1 ♭5

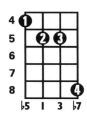
♭5 1 3 ♭7

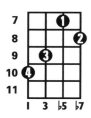
1 3 ♭5 ♭7

## C7+5
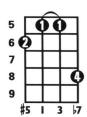
#5 1 3 ♭7

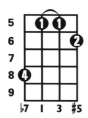
♭7 1 3 #5

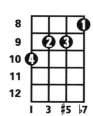
1 3 #5 ♭7

## C7-9
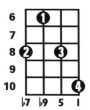
♭7 ♭9 5 1

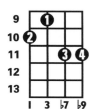
1 3 ♭7 ♭9

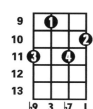
♭9 3 ♭7 1

## C7+9
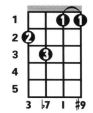
3 ♭7 1 #9

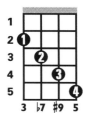
3 ♭7 #9 5

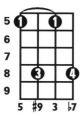
5 #9 3 ♭7

# C Chords

## Cm(maj7)

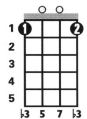
♭3 5 7 ♭3

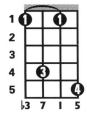
♭3 7 I 5

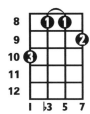
I ♭3 5 7

## Cmaj7-5

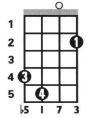
♭5 I 7 3

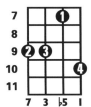
7 3 ♭5 I

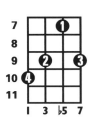
I 3 ♭5 7

## Cmaj7+5

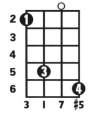
3 I 7 #5

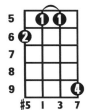
#5 I 3 7

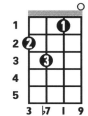
I 3 #5 7

## C9

3 ♭7 I 9

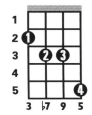
3 ♭7 9 5

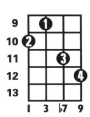
I 3 ♭7 9

## Cm9

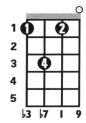
♭3 ♭7 I 9

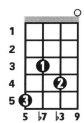
5 ♭7 ♭3 9

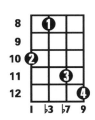
I ♭3 ♭7 9

## Cmaj9

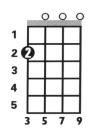
3 5 7 9

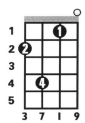
3 7 I 9

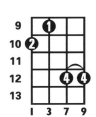
I 3 7 9

## C11

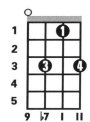
9 ♭7 I II

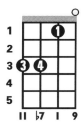
II ♭7 I 9

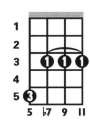
5 ♭7 9 II

## C13

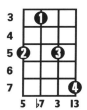
5 ♭7 3 13

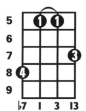
♭7 I 3 13

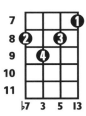
♭7 3 5 13

15

# C Chords (Advanced)

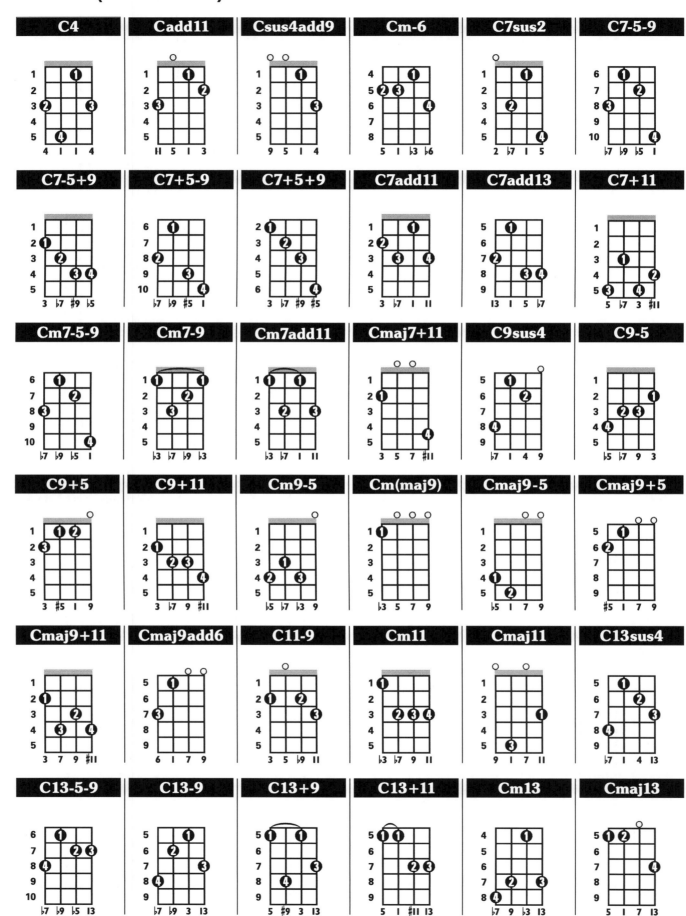

## D♭

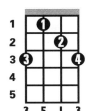

## D♭m

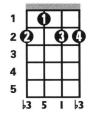

## D♭7

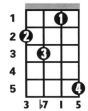

## D♭m7

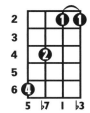

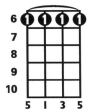

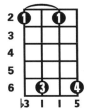

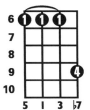

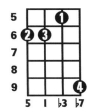

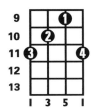

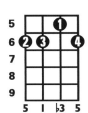

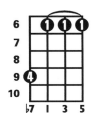

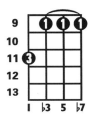

## D♭5

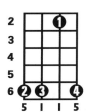

## D♭6

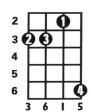

## D♭m6

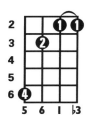

## D♭maj7

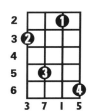

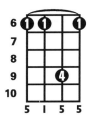

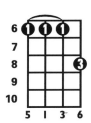

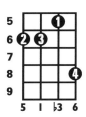

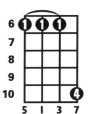

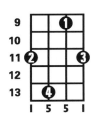

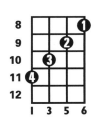

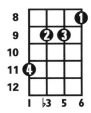

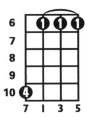

# C#/ D♭ Chords

| D♭° | D♭°7 | D♭-5 | D♭+ |
|---|---|---|---|

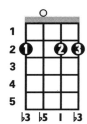
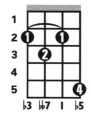
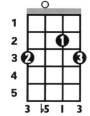
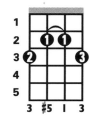

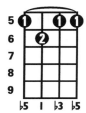
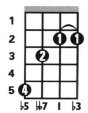
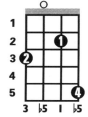
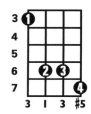

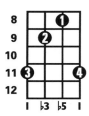
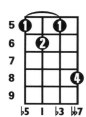
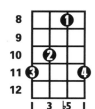
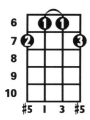

| D♭sus2 | D♭sus4 | D♭7sus4 | D♭m7-5 |
|---|---|---|---|

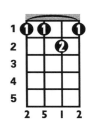
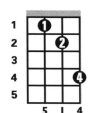
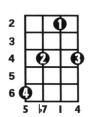
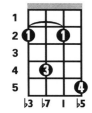

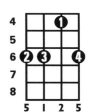
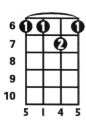
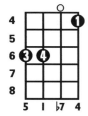
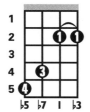

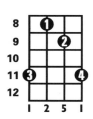
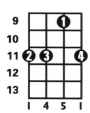
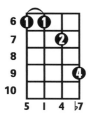
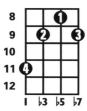

## D♭add9

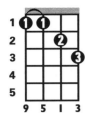
9 5 1 3

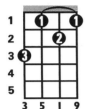
3 5 1 9

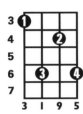
3 1 9 5

## D♭madd9

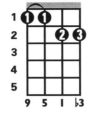
9 5 1 ♭3

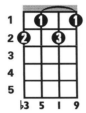
♭3 5 1 9

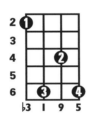
♭3 1 9 5

## D♭6add9

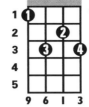
9 6 1 3

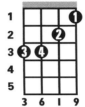
3 6 1 9

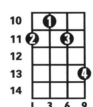
1 3 6 9

## D♭m6add9

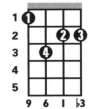
9 6 1 ♭3

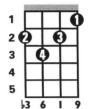
♭3 6 1 9

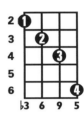
♭3 6 9 5

## D♭7-5

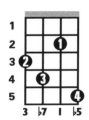
3 ♭7 1 ♭5

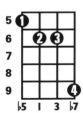
♭5 1 3 ♭7

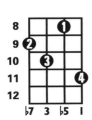
♭7 3 ♭5 1

## D♭7+5

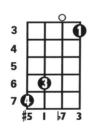
#5 1 ♭7 3

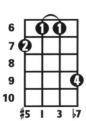
#5 1 3 ♭7

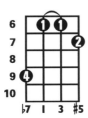
♭7 1 3 #5

## D♭7-9

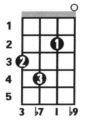
3 ♭7 1 ♭9

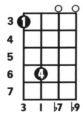
3 1 ♭7 ♭9

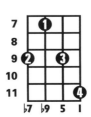
♭7 ♭9 5 1

## D♭7+9

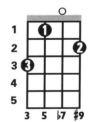
3 5 ♭7 #9

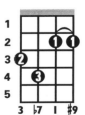
3 ♭7 1 #9

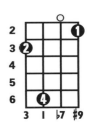
3 1 ♭7 #9

# C#/ D♭ Chords

## D♭m(maj7)

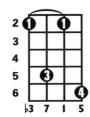

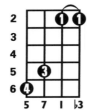

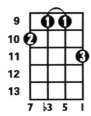

## D♭maj7-5

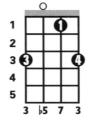

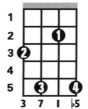

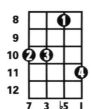

## D♭maj7+5

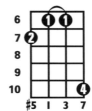

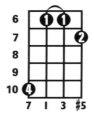

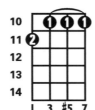

## D♭9

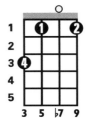

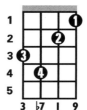

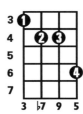

## D♭m9

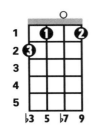

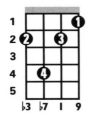

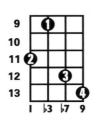

## D♭maj9

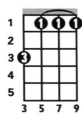

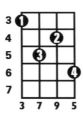

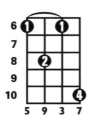

## D♭11

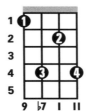

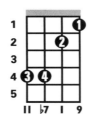

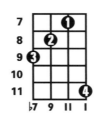

## D♭13

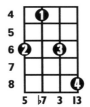

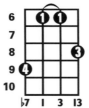

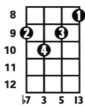

# C#/ D♭ Chords (Advanced)

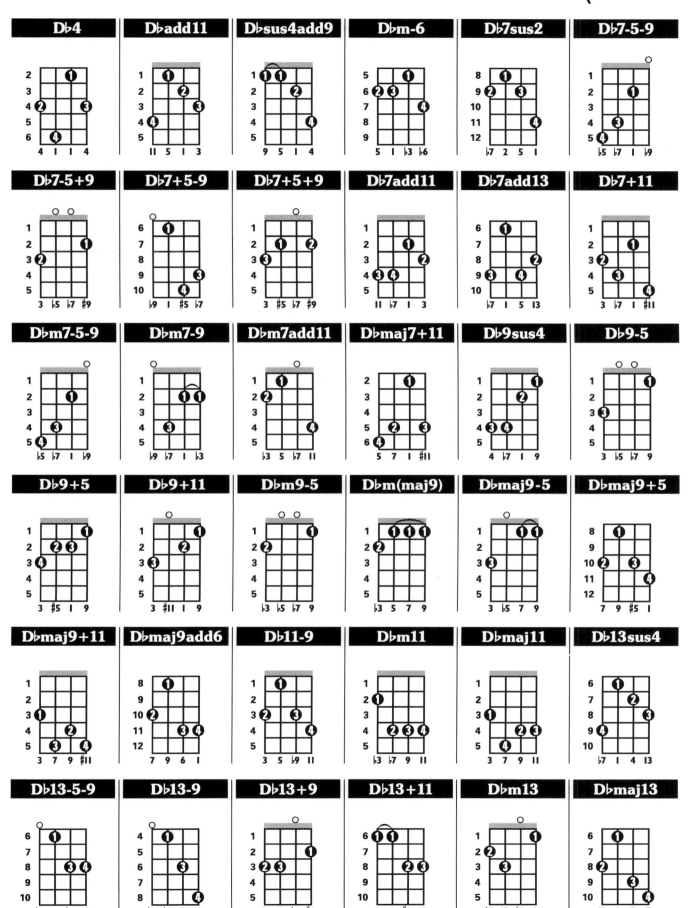

# D Chords

| D | Dm | D7 | Dm7 |
|---|---|---|---|

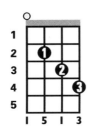
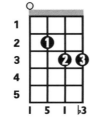
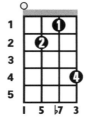
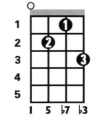

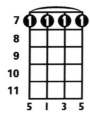
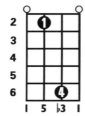
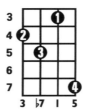
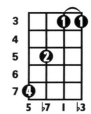

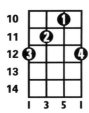
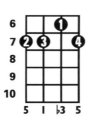
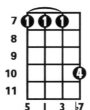
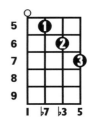

| D5 | D6 | Dm6 | Dmaj7 |
|---|---|---|---|

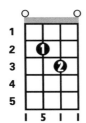
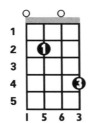
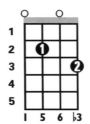
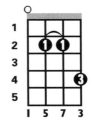

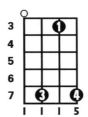
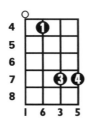
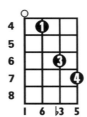
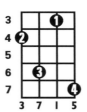

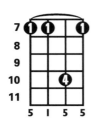
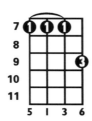
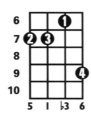
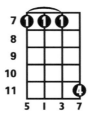

# D Chords

## D°

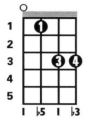

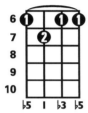

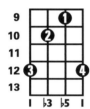

## D°7

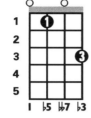

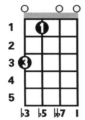

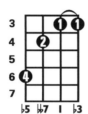

## D-5

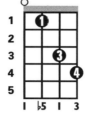

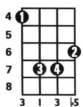

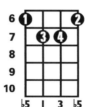

## D+

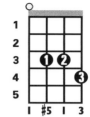

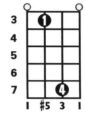

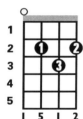

## Dsus2

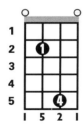

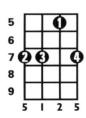

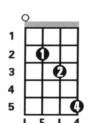

## Dsus4

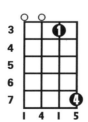

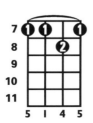

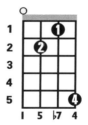

## D7sus4

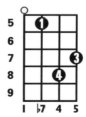

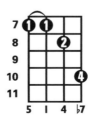

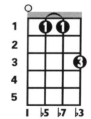

## Dm7-5

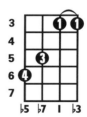

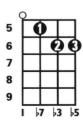

# D Chords

## Dadd9
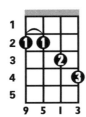
9 5 1 3

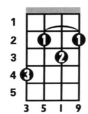
3 5 1 9

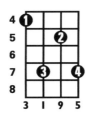
3 1 9 5

## Dmadd9
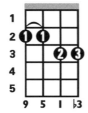
9 5 1 ♭3

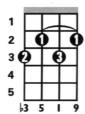
♭3 5 1 9

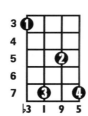
♭3 1 9 5

## D6add9
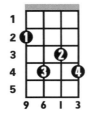
9 6 1 3

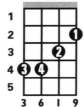
3 6 1 9

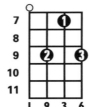
1 9 3 6

## Dm6add9
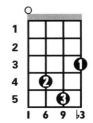
1 6 9 ♭3

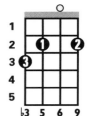
♭3 5 6 9

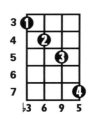
♭3 6 9 5

## D7-5
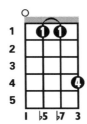
1 ♭5 ♭7 3

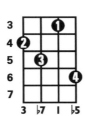
3 ♭7 1 ♭5

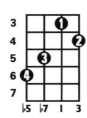
♭5 ♭7 1 3

## D7+5
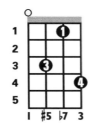
1 #5 ♭7 3

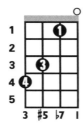
3 #5 ♭7 1

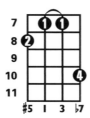
#5 1 3 ♭7

## D7-9
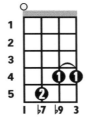
1 ♭7 ♭9 3

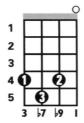
3 ♭7 ♭9 1

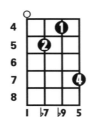
1 ♭7 ♭9 5

## D7+9
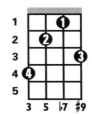
3 5 ♭7 #9

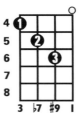
3 ♭7 #9 1

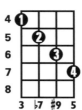
3 ♭7 #9 5

# D Chords

## Dm(maj7)
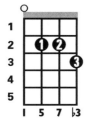
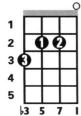
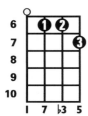

## Dmaj7-5
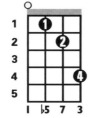
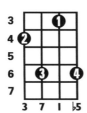

## Dmaj7+5
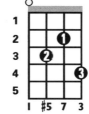
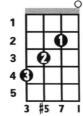

## D9
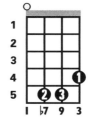
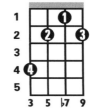
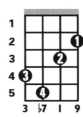

## Dm9
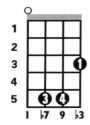
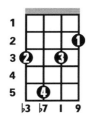
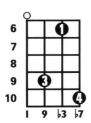

## Dmaj9
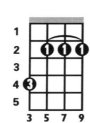
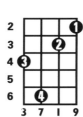
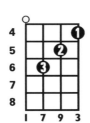

## D11
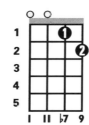
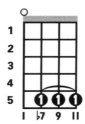
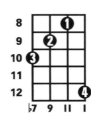

## D13
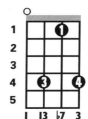
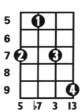
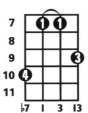

25

# D Chords (Advanced)

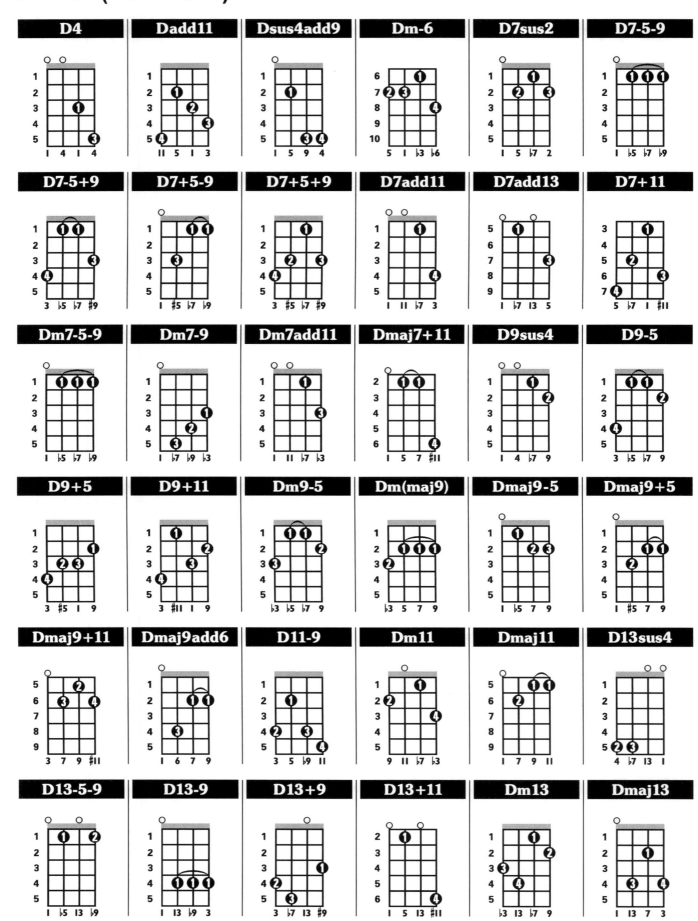

## E♭
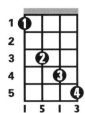
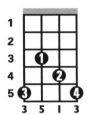
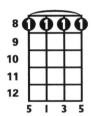

## E♭m
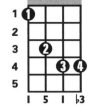
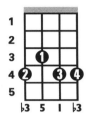
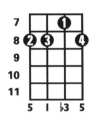

## E♭7
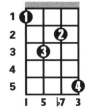
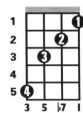
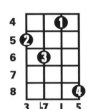

## E♭m7
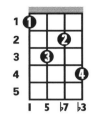
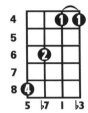
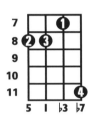

## E♭5
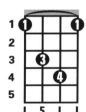
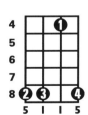
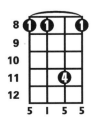

## E♭6
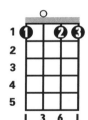
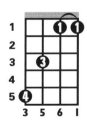
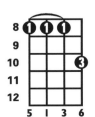

## E♭m6
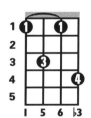
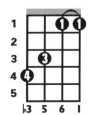
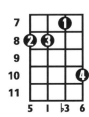

## E♭maj7
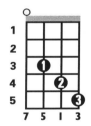
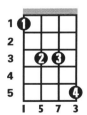
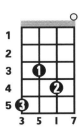

# D#/ E♭ Chords

| E♭° | E♭°7 | E♭-5 | E♭+ |
|---|---|---|---|

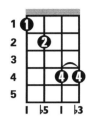
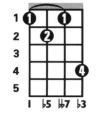
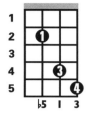
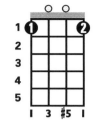

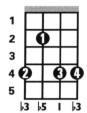
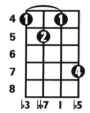
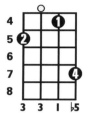
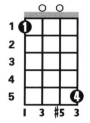

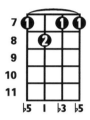
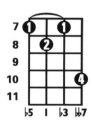
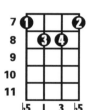
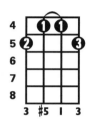

| E♭sus2 | E♭sus4 | E♭7sus4 | E♭m7-5 |
|---|---|---|---|

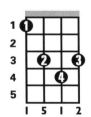
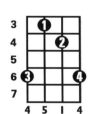
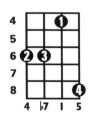
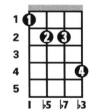

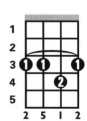
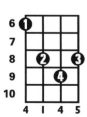
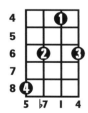
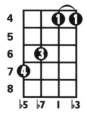

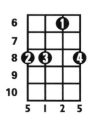
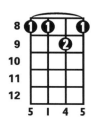
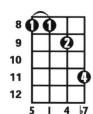
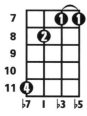

## E♭add9

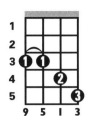
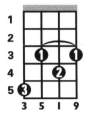
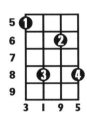

## E♭madd9

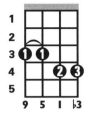
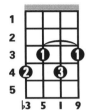
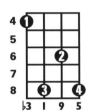

## E♭6add9

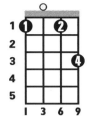
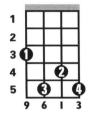
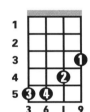

## E♭m6add9

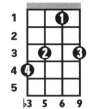
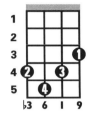
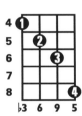

## E♭7-5

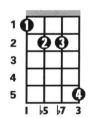
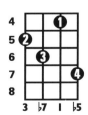
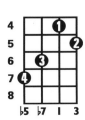

## E♭7+5

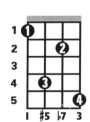
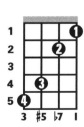
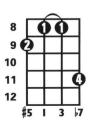

## E♭7-9

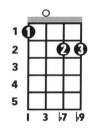
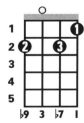
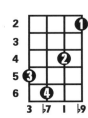

## E♭7+9

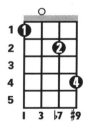
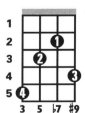
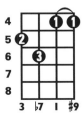

# D#/ E♭ Chords

| E♭m(maj7) | E♭maj7-5 | E♭maj7+5 | E♭9 |
|---|---|---|---|

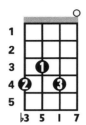
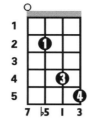
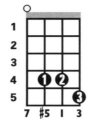
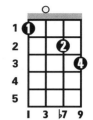

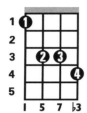
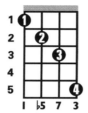
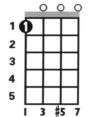
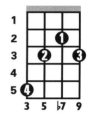

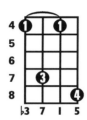
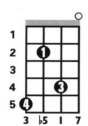
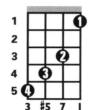
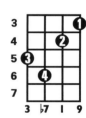

| E♭m9 | E♭maj9 | E♭11 | E♭13 |
|---|---|---|---|

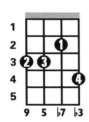
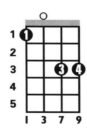
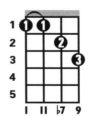
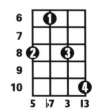

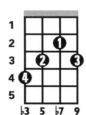
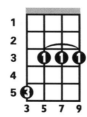
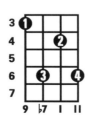
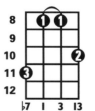

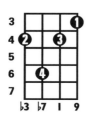
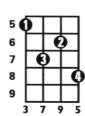
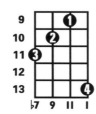
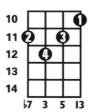

# D#/ E♭ Chords (Advanced)

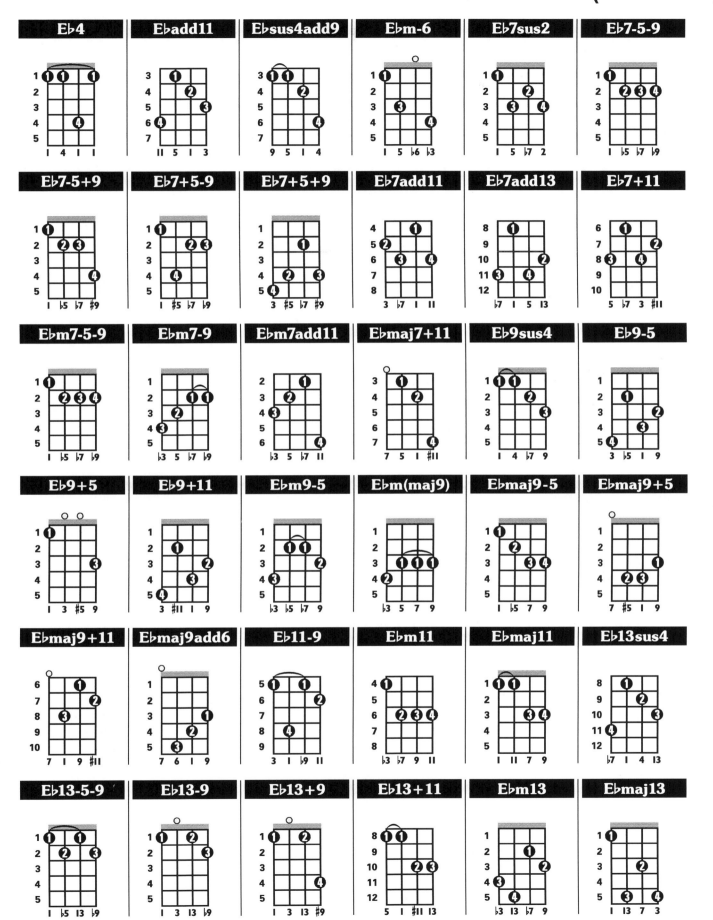

# E Chords

| E | Em | E7 | Em7 |
|---|---|---|---|

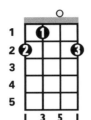
I 3 5 I

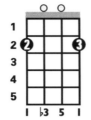
I ♭3 5 I

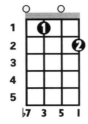
♭7 3 5 I

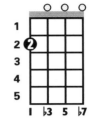
I ♭3 5 ♭7

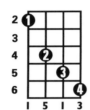
I 5 I 3

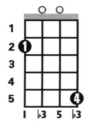
I ♭3 5 ♭3

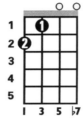
I 3 5 ♭7

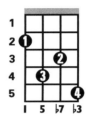
I 5 ♭7 ♭3

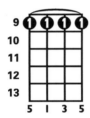
5 I 3 5

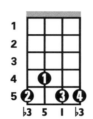
♭3 5 I ♭3

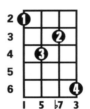
I 5 ♭7 3

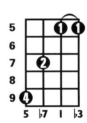
5 ♭7 I ♭3

| E5 | E6 | Em6 | Emaj7 |
|---|---|---|---|

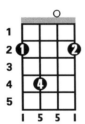
I 5 5 I

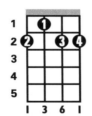
I 3 6 I

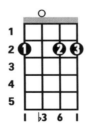
I ♭3 6 I

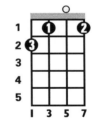
I 3 5 7

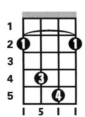
I 5 I I

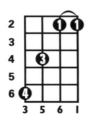
3 5 6 I

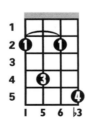
I 5 6 ♭3

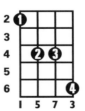
I 5 7 3

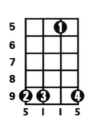
5 I I 5

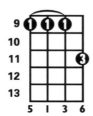
5 I 3 6

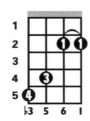
♭3 5 6 I

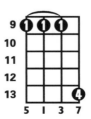
5 I 3 7

# E Chords

## E°

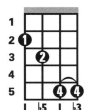

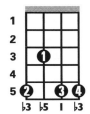

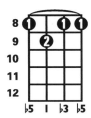

## E°7

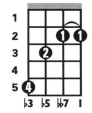

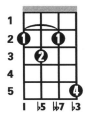

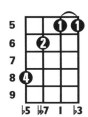

## E-5

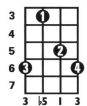

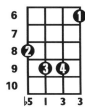

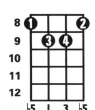

## E+

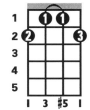

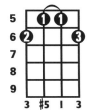

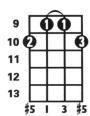

## Esus2

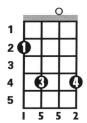

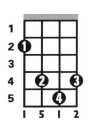

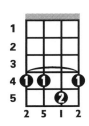

## Esus4

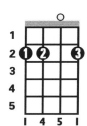

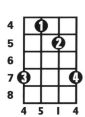

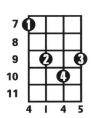

## E7sus4

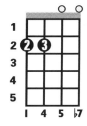

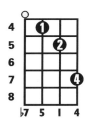

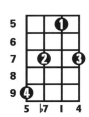

## Em7-5

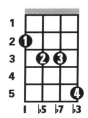

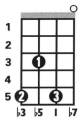

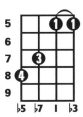

33

# E Chords

## Eadd9
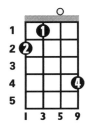
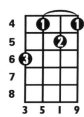
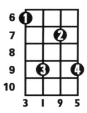

## Emadd9
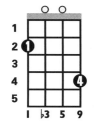
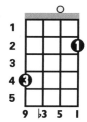
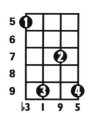

## E6add9
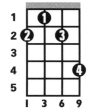
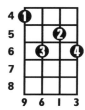
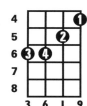

## Em6add9
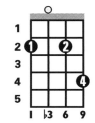
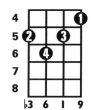
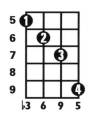

## E7-5
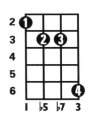
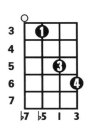
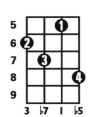

## E7+5
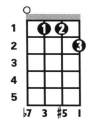
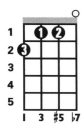
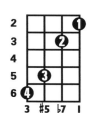

## E7-9
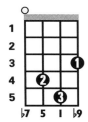
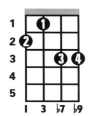
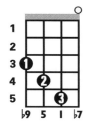

## E7+9
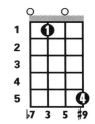
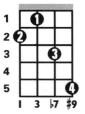
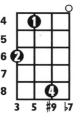

# E Chords

## Em(maj7)

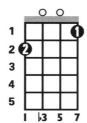

I ♭3 5 7

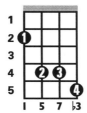

I 5 7 ♭3

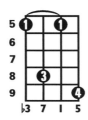

♭3 7 I 5

## Emaj7-5

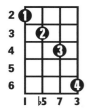

I ♭5 7 3

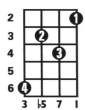

3 ♭5 7 I

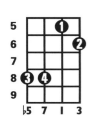

♭5 7 I 3

## Emaj7+5

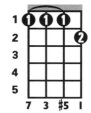

7 3 #5 I

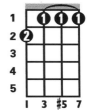

I 3 #5 7

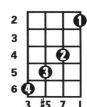

3 #5 7 I

## E9

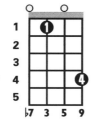

♭7 3 5 9

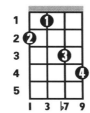

I 3 ♭7 9

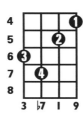

3 ♭7 I 9

## Em9

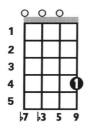

♭7 ♭3 5 9

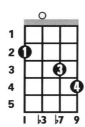

I ♭3 ♭7 9

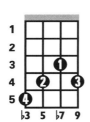

♭3 5 ♭7 9

## Emaj9

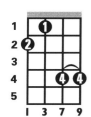

I 3 7 9

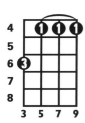

3 5 7 9

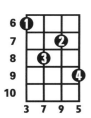

3 7 9 5

## E11

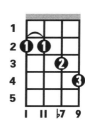

I II ♭7 9

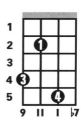

9 II I ♭7

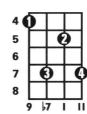

9 ♭7 I II

## E13

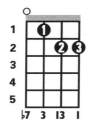

♭7 3 13 I

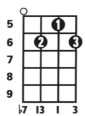

♭7 13 I 3

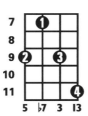

5 ♭7 3 13

35

# E Chords (Advanced)

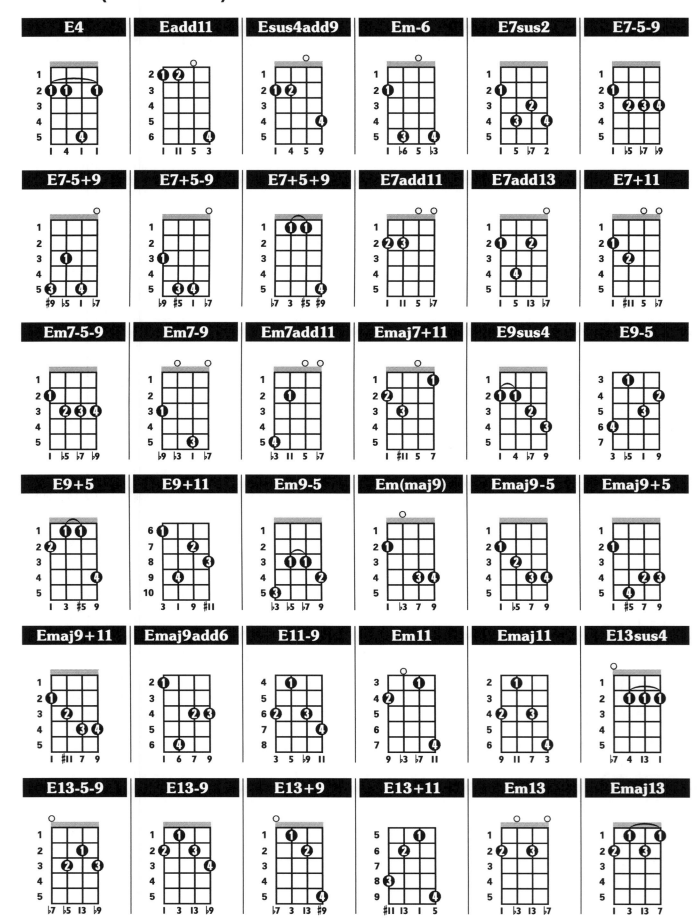

# F Chords

**F**

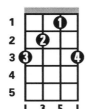

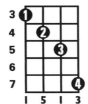

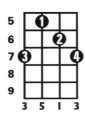

**Fm**

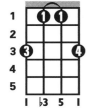

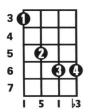

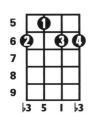

**F7**

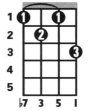

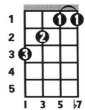

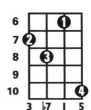

**Fm7**

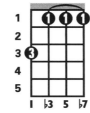

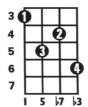

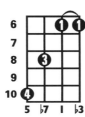

**F5**

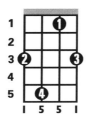

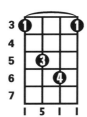

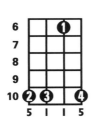

**F6**

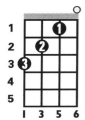

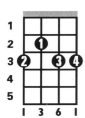

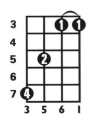

**Fm6**

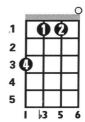

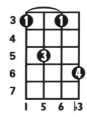

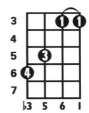

**Fmaj7**

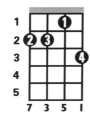

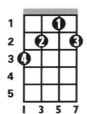

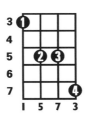

# F Chords

## F°

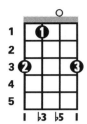

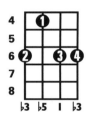

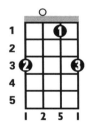

## F°7

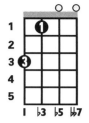

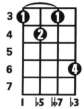

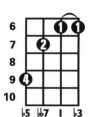

## F-5

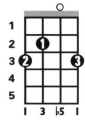

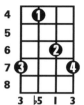

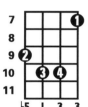

## F+

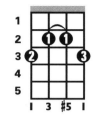

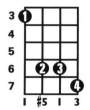

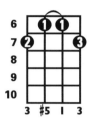

## Fsus2

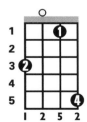

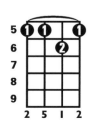

## Fsus4

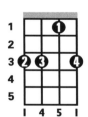

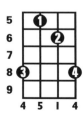

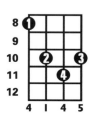

## F7sus4

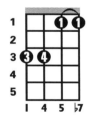

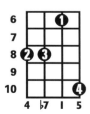

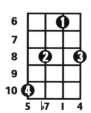

## Fm7-5

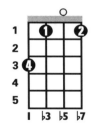

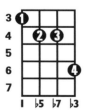

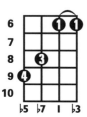

# F Chords

**Fadd9**

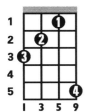

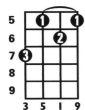

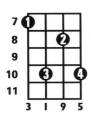

**Fmadd9**

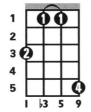

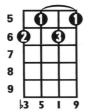

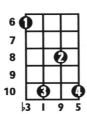

**F6add9**

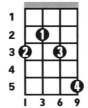

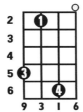

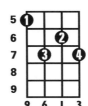

**Fm6add9**

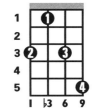

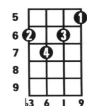

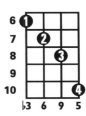

**F7-5**

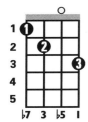

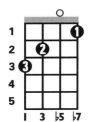

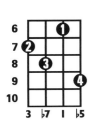

**F7+5**

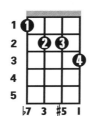

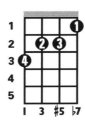

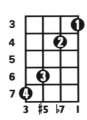

**F7-9**

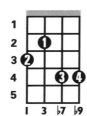

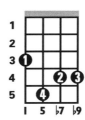

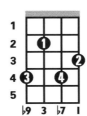

**F7+9**

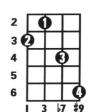

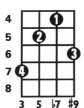

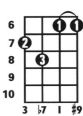

# F Chords

| Fm(maj7) | Fmaj7-5 | Fmaj7+5 | F9 |
|---|---|---|---|
| 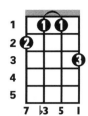 | 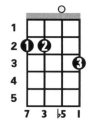 | 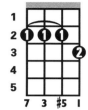 | 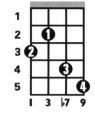 |
| 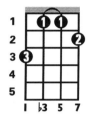 | 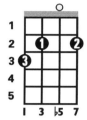 | 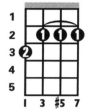 | 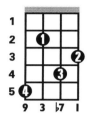 |
| 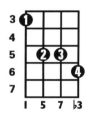 | 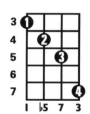 | 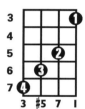 | 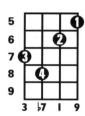 |

| Fm9 | Fmaj9 | F11 | F13 |
|---|---|---|---|
| 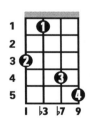 | 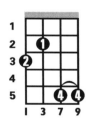 | 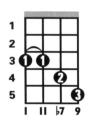 | 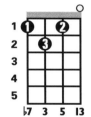 |
| 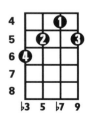 | 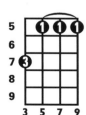 | 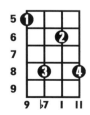 | 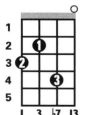 |
| 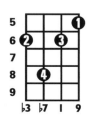 | 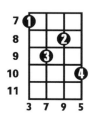 | 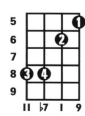 | 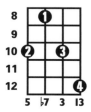 |

40

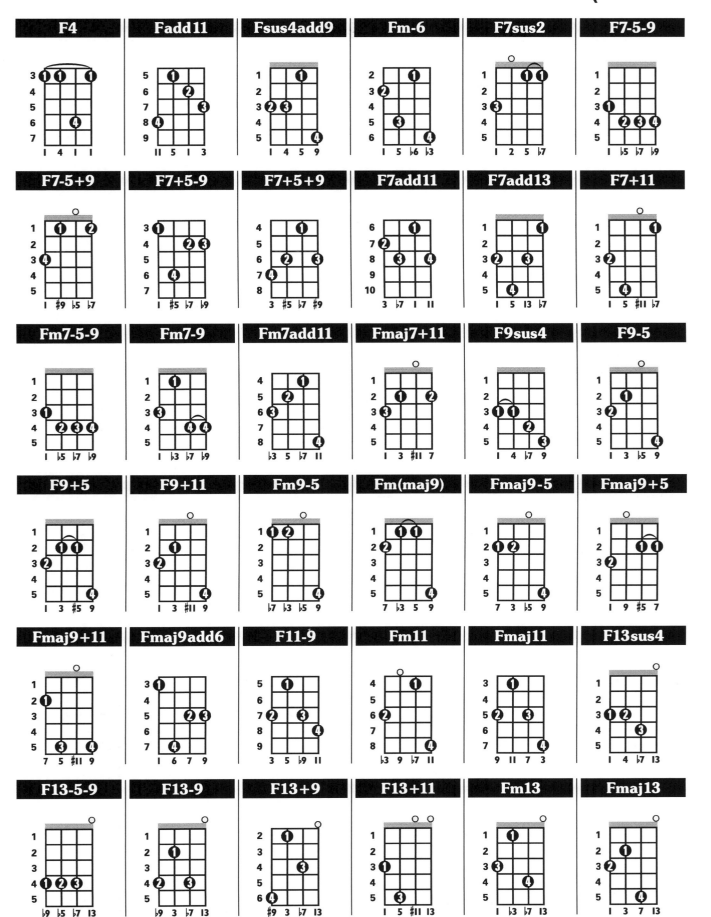

# F♯/ G♭ Chords

| F# | F#m | F#7 | F#m7 |
|---|---|---|---|

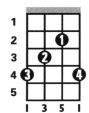
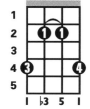
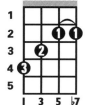
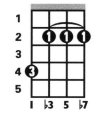

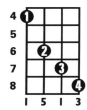
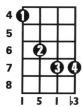
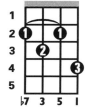
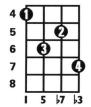

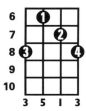
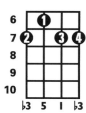
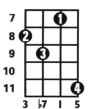
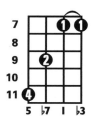

| F#5 | F#6 | F#m6 | F#maj7 |
|---|---|---|---|

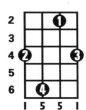
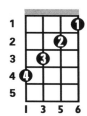
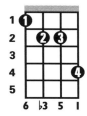
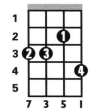

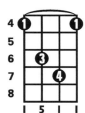
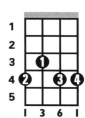
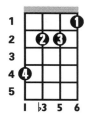
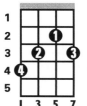

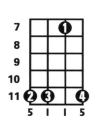
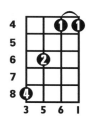
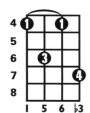
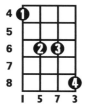

**F#°**

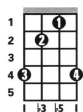

**F#°7**

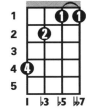

**F#-5**

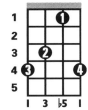

**F#+**

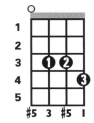

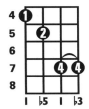

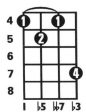

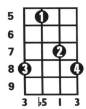

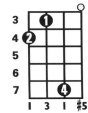

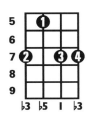

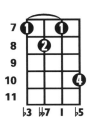

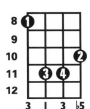

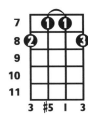

**F#sus2**

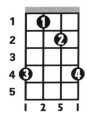

**F#sus4**

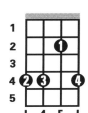

**F#7sus4**

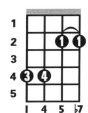

**F#m7-5**

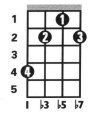

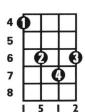

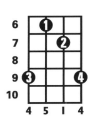

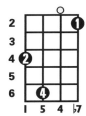

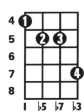

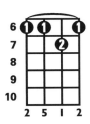

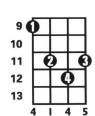

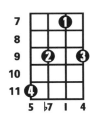

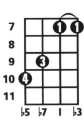

# F# / Gb Chords

## F#add9
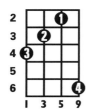
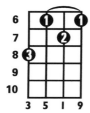
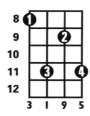

## F#madd9
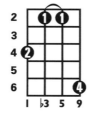
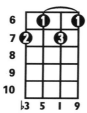
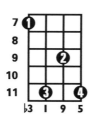

## F#6add9
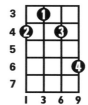
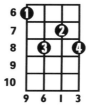
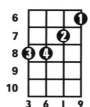

## F#m6add9
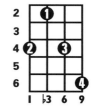
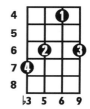
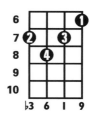

## F#7-5
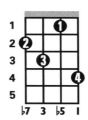
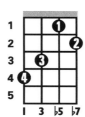
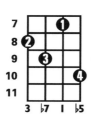

## F#7+5
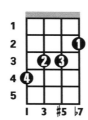
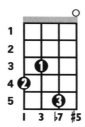
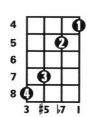

## F#7-9
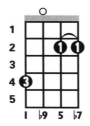
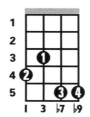
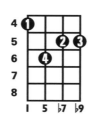

## F#7+9
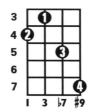
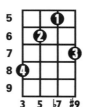
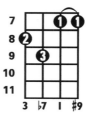

## F#m(maj7)

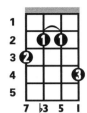
7  ♭3  5  1

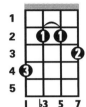
1  ♭3  5  7

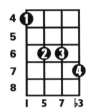
1  5  7  ♭3

## F#maj7-5

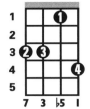
7  3  ♭5  1

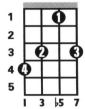
1  3  ♭5  7

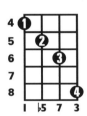
1  ♭5  7  3

## F#maj7+5

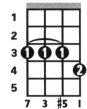
7  3  #5  1

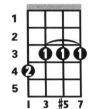
1  3  #5  7

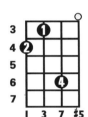
1  3  7  #5

## F#9

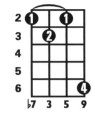
♭7  3  5  9

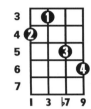
1  3  ♭7  9

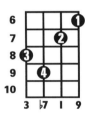
3  ♭7  1  9

## F#m9

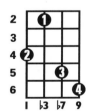
1  ♭3  ♭7  9

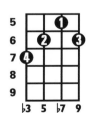
♭3  5  ♭7  9

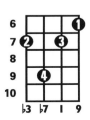
♭3  ♭7  1  9

## F#maj9

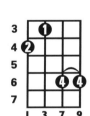
1  3  7  9

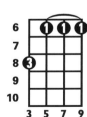
3  5  7  9

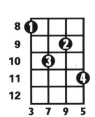
3  7  9  5

## F#11

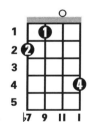
♭7  9  11  1

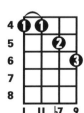
1  11  ♭7  9

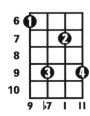
9  ♭7  1  11

## F#13

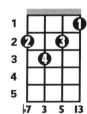
♭7  3  5  13

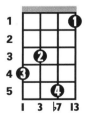
1  3  ♭7  13

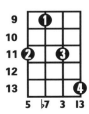
5  ♭7  ♭9  13

# F#/ Gb Chords (Advanced)

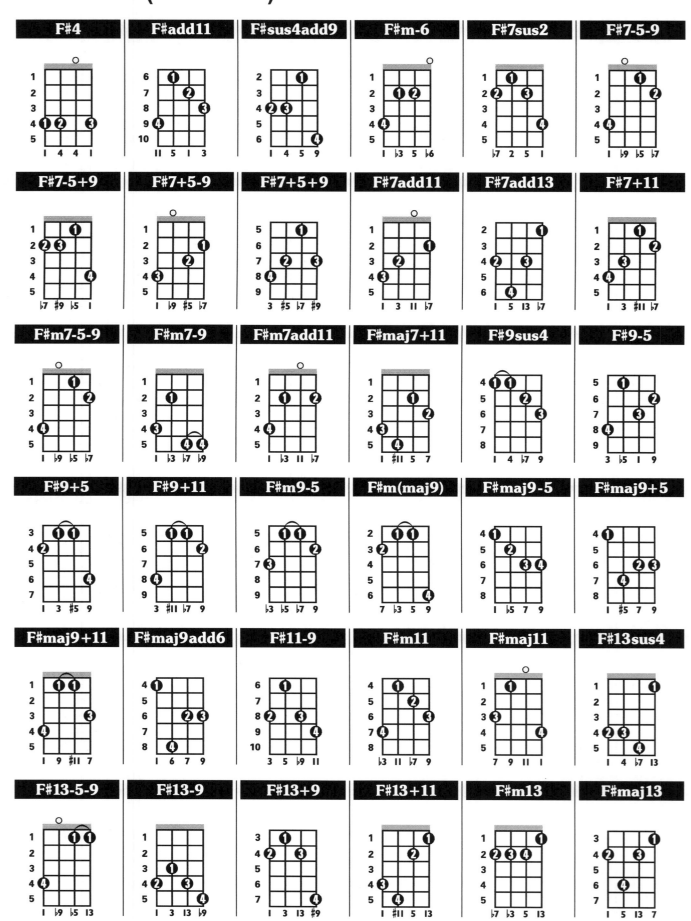

# G Chords

| G | Gm | G7 | Gm7 |
|---|---|---|---|

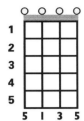
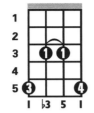
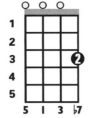
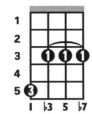

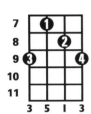
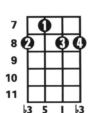
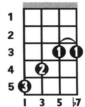
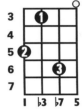

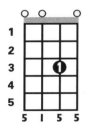
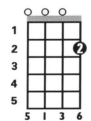
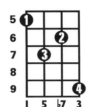
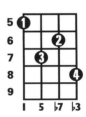

| G5 | G6 | Gm6 | Gmaj7 |
|---|---|---|---|

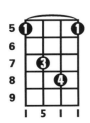
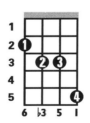
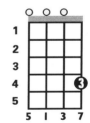

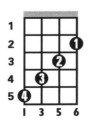
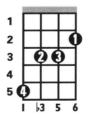
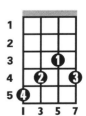

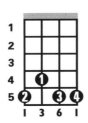
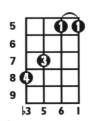
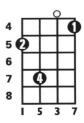

# G Chords

| Gº | Gº7 | G-5 | G+ |
|---|---|---|---|

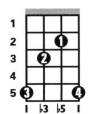 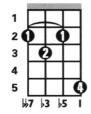 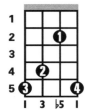 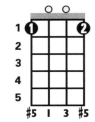

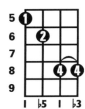 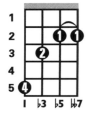 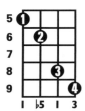 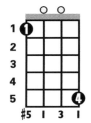

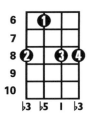 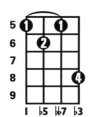 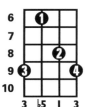 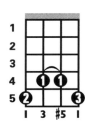

| Gsus2 | Gsus4 | G7sus4 | Gm7-5 |
|---|---|---|---|

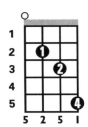 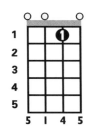 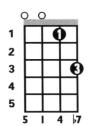 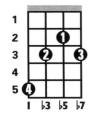

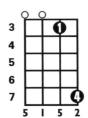 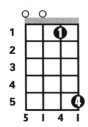 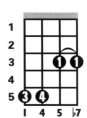 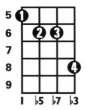

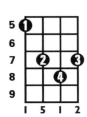 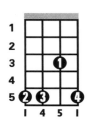 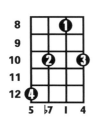 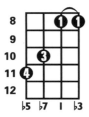

# G Chords

## Gadd9

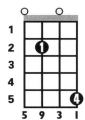

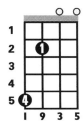

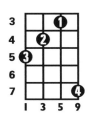

## Gmadd9

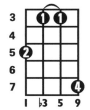

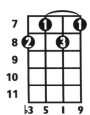

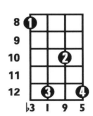

## G6add9

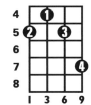

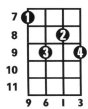

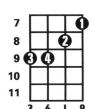

## Gm6add9

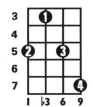

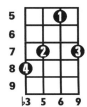

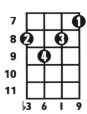

## G7-5

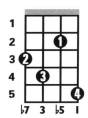

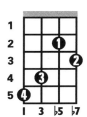

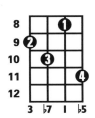

## G7+5

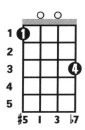

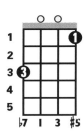

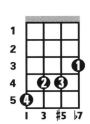

## G7-9

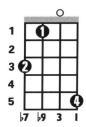

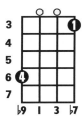

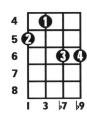

## G7+9

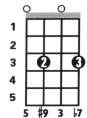

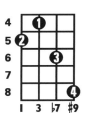

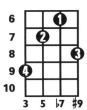

49

# G Chords

| Gm(maj7) | Gmaj7-5 | Gmaj7+5 | G9 |
|---|---|---|---|

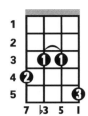 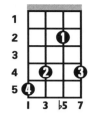 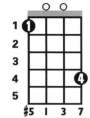 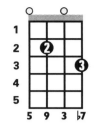

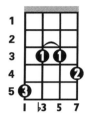 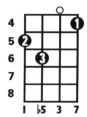 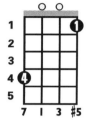 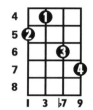

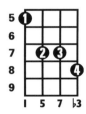 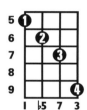 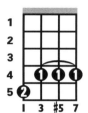 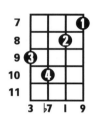

| Gm9 | Gmaj9 | G11 | G13 |
|---|---|---|---|

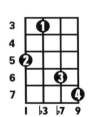 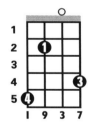 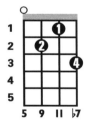 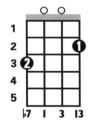

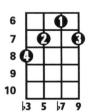 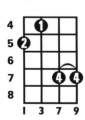 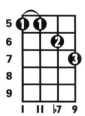 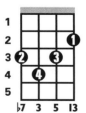

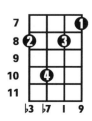 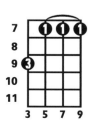 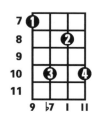 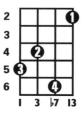

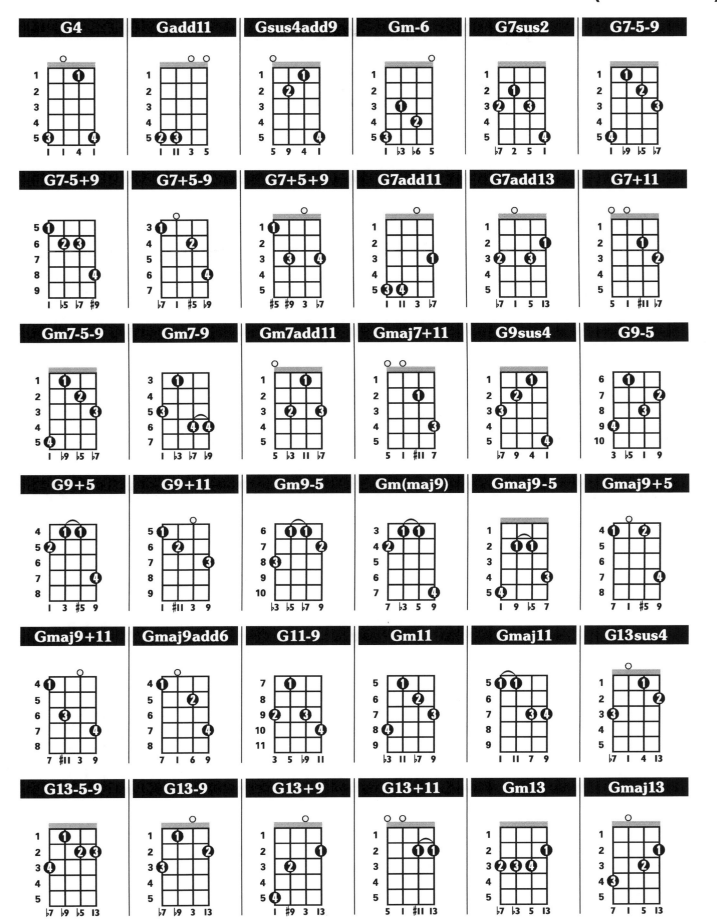

# G#/A♭ Chords

| A♭ | A♭m | A♭7 | A♭m7 |
|---|---|---|---|

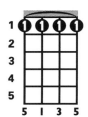 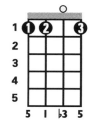 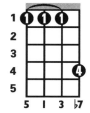 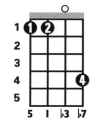

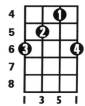 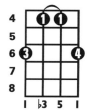 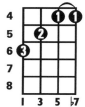 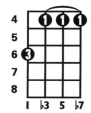

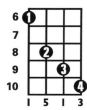 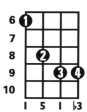 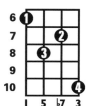 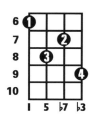

| A♭5 | A♭6 | A♭m6 | A♭maj7 |
|---|---|---|---|

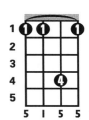 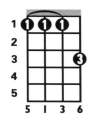 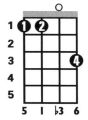 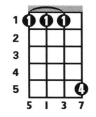

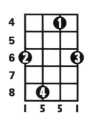 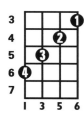 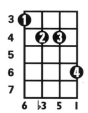 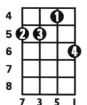

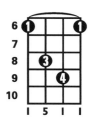 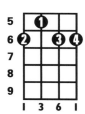 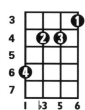 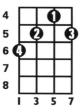

## A♭°

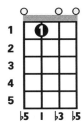

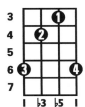

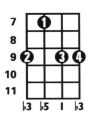

## A♭°7

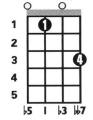

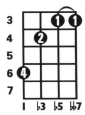

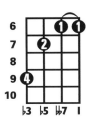

## A♭-5

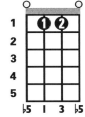

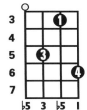

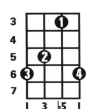

## A♭+

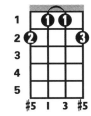

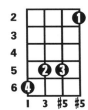

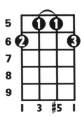

## A♭sus2

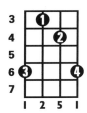

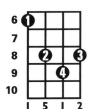

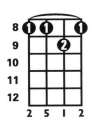

## A♭sus4

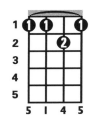

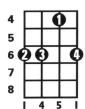

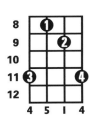

## A♭7sus4

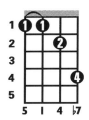

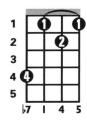

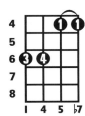

## A♭m7-5

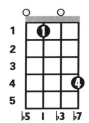

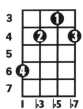

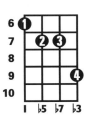

# G#/A♭ Chords

## A♭add9

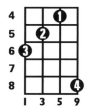

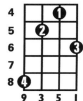

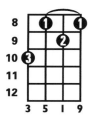

## A♭madd9

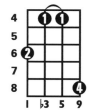

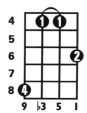

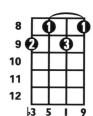

## A♭6add9

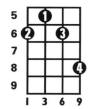

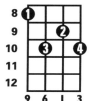

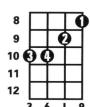

## A♭m6add9

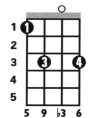

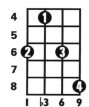

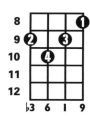

## A♭7-5

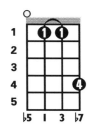

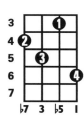

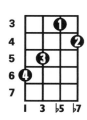

## A♭7+5

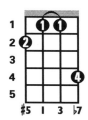

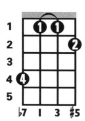

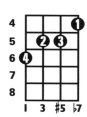

## A♭7-9

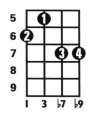

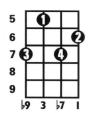

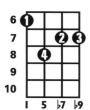

## A♭7+9

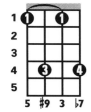

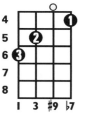

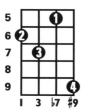

54

## A♭m(maj7)
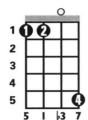
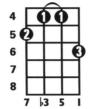
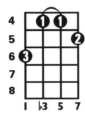

## A♭maj7-5
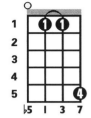
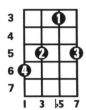
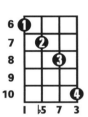

## A♭maj7+5
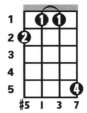
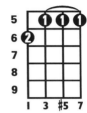
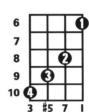

## A♭9
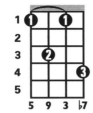
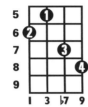
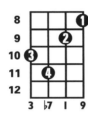

## A♭m9
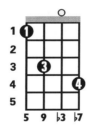
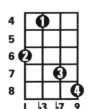
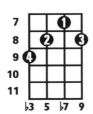

## A♭maj9
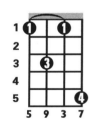
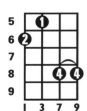
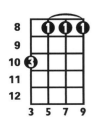

## A♭11
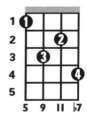
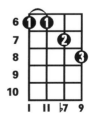
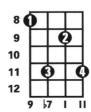

## A♭13
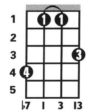
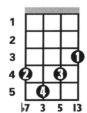
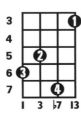

# G# / A♭ Chords (Advanced)

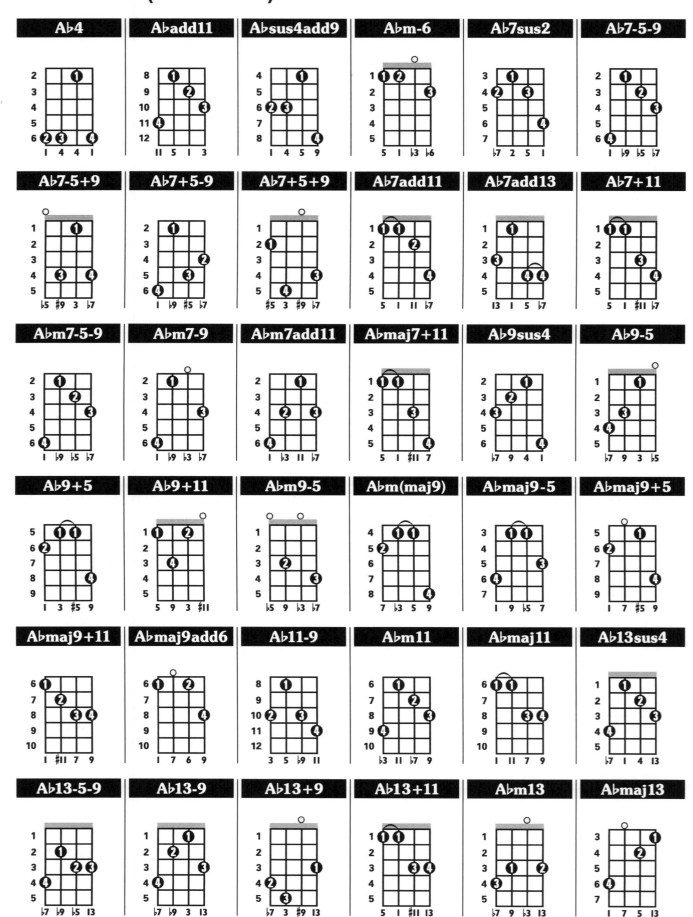

# A Chords

| A | Am | A7 | Am7 |
|---|----|----|----|

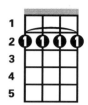 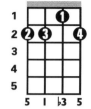 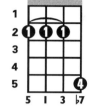 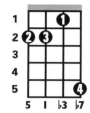

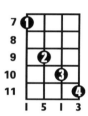 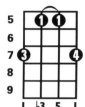 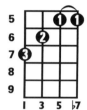 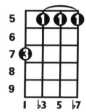

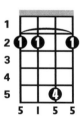 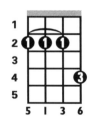 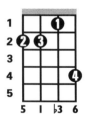 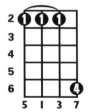

| A5 | A6 | Am6 | Amaj7 |
|----|----|-----|-------|

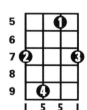 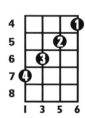 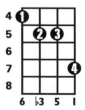 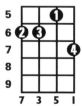

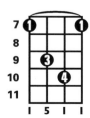 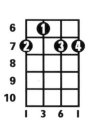 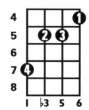 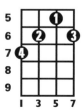

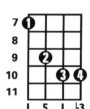 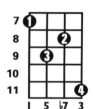 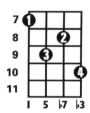

# A Chords

| A° | A°7 | A-5 | A+ |
|---|---|---|---|

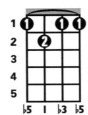
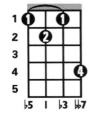
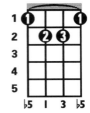
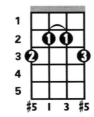

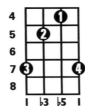
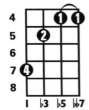
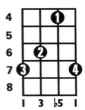
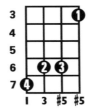

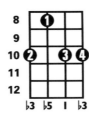
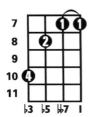
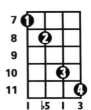
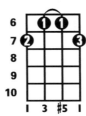

| Asus2 | Asus4 | A7sus4 | Am7-5 |
|---|---|---|---|

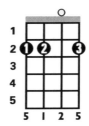
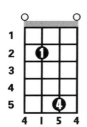
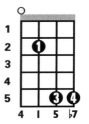
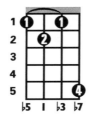

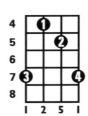
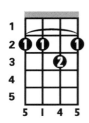
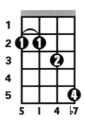
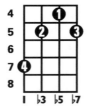

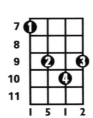
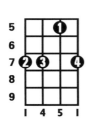
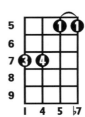
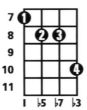

## Aadd9

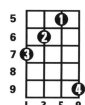

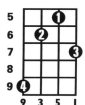

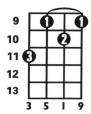

## Amadd9

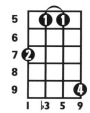

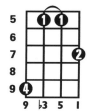

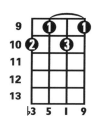

## A6add9

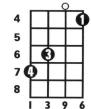

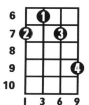

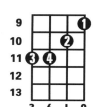

## Am6add9

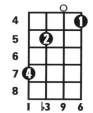

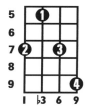

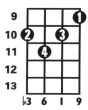

## A7-5

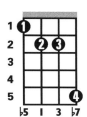

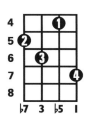

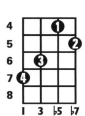

## A7+5

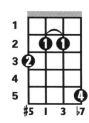

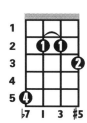

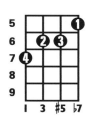

## A7-9

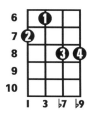

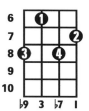

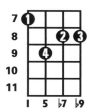

## A7+9

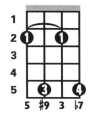

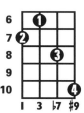

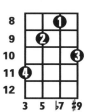

# A Chords

## Am(maj7)

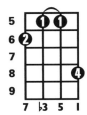

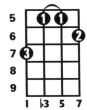

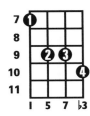

## Amaj7-5

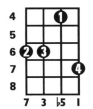

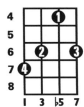

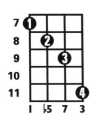

## Amaj7+5

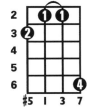

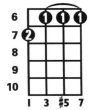

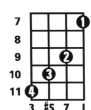

## A9

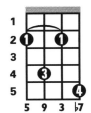

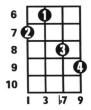

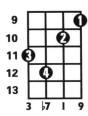

## Am9

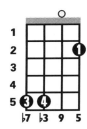

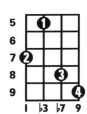

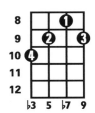

## Amaj9

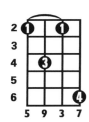

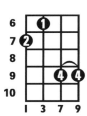

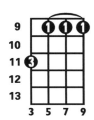

## A11

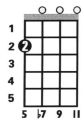

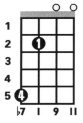

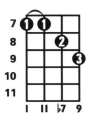

## A13

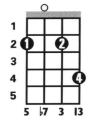

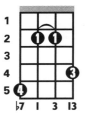

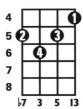

# A Chords (Advanced)

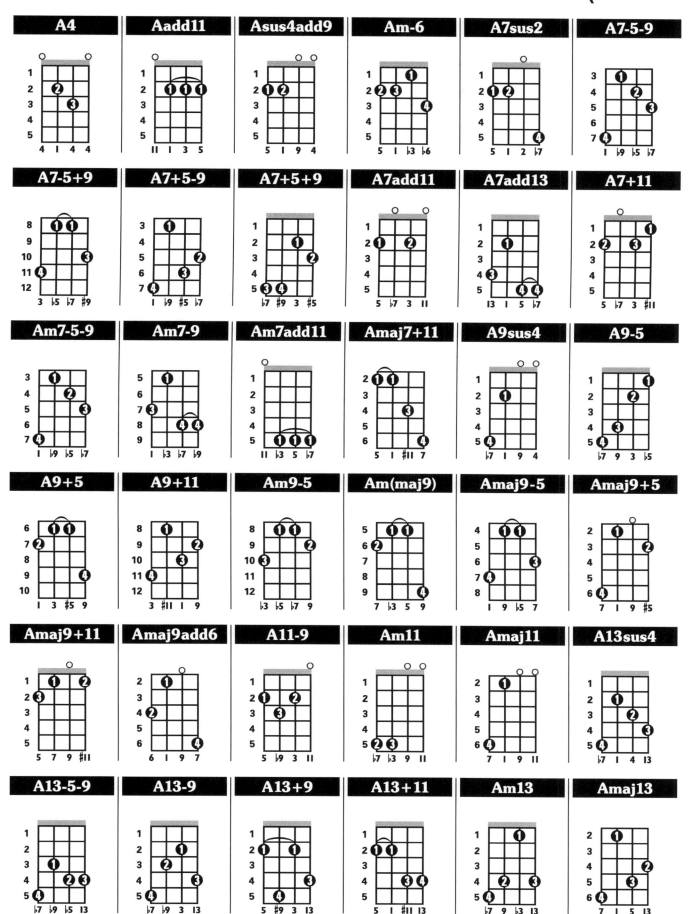

# A# / B♭ Chords

| B♭ | B♭m | B♭7 | B♭m7 |
|---|---|---|---|

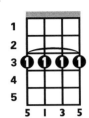
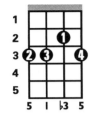
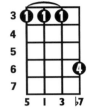
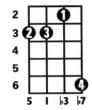

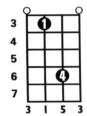
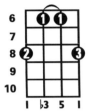
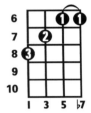
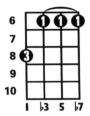

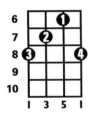
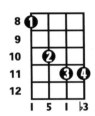
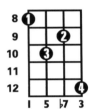
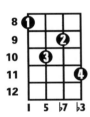

| B♭5 | B♭6 | B♭m6 | B♭maj7 |
|---|---|---|---|

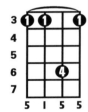
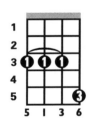
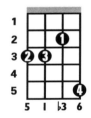
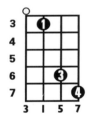

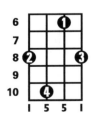
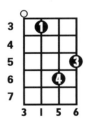
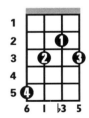
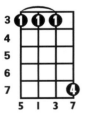

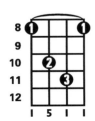
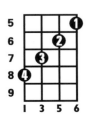
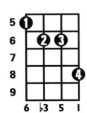
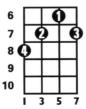

**B♭o**

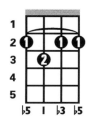

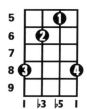

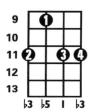

**B♭o7**

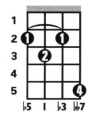

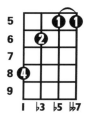

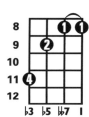

**B♭-5**

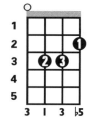

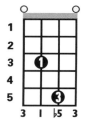

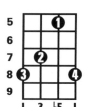

**B♭+**

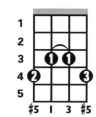

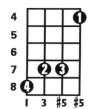

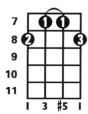

**B♭sus2**

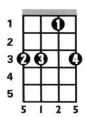

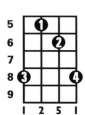

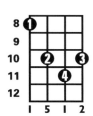

**B♭sus4**

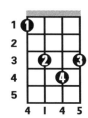

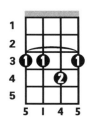

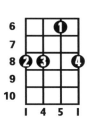

**B♭7sus4**

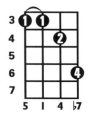

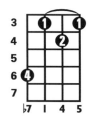

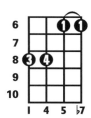

**B♭m7-5**

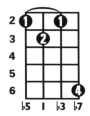

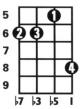

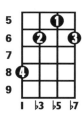

# A# / B♭ Chords

| B♭add9 | B♭madd9 | B♭6add9 | B♭m6add9 |
|---|---|---|---|

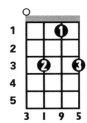

3 1 9 5

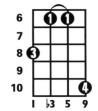

I ♭3 5 9

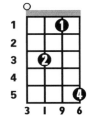

3 1 9 6

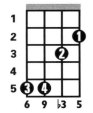

6 9 ♭3 5

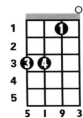

5 1 9 3

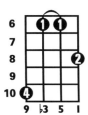

9 ♭3 5 I

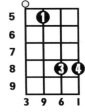

3 9 6 I

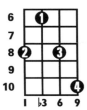

I ♭3 6 9

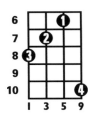

I 3 5 9

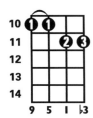

9 5 I ♭3

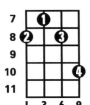

I 3 6 9

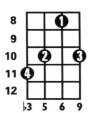

♭3 5 6 9

| B♭7-5 | B♭7+5 | B♭7-9 | B♭7+9 |
|---|---|---|---|

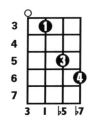

3 1 ♭5 ♭7

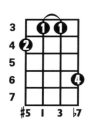

#5 I 3 ♭7

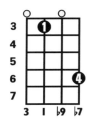

3 1 ♭9 ♭7

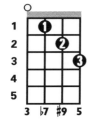

3 ♭7 #9 5

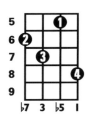

♭7 3 ♭5 I

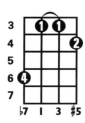

♭7 I 3 #5

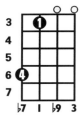

♭7 I ♭9 3

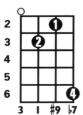

3 I #9 ♭7

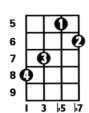

I 3 ♭5 ♭7

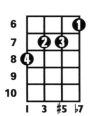

I 3 #5 ♭7

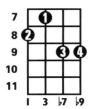

I 3 ♭7 ♭9

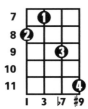

I 3 ♭7 #9

# A#/ B♭ Chords

## B♭m(maj7)

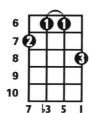

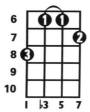

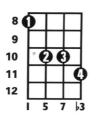

## B♭maj7-5

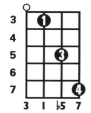

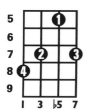

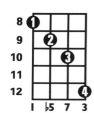

## B♭maj7+5

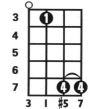

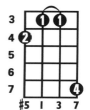

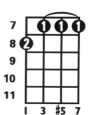

## B♭9

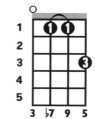

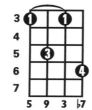

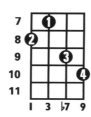

## B♭m9

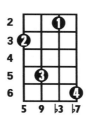

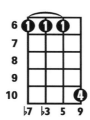

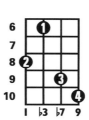

## B♭maj9

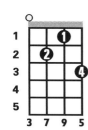

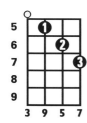

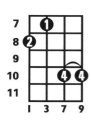

## B♭11

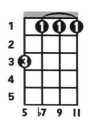

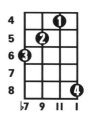

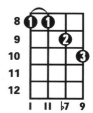

## B♭13

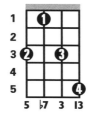

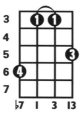

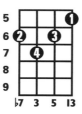

# A# / B♭ Chords (Advanced)

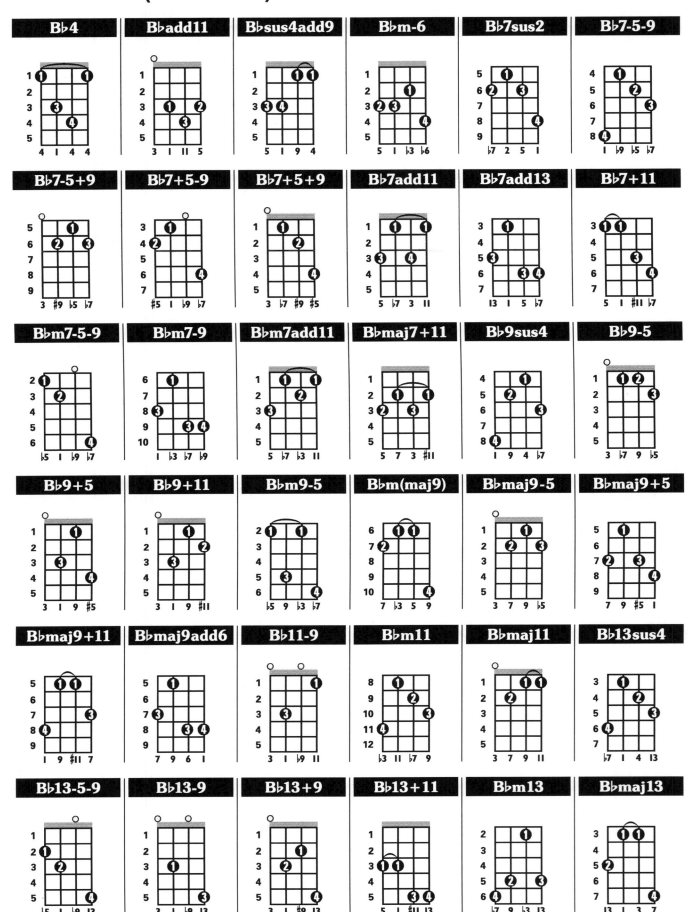

# B Chords

## B
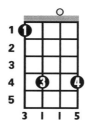
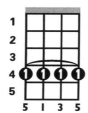
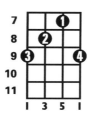

## Bm
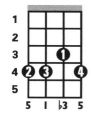
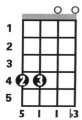
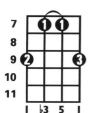

## B7
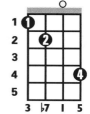
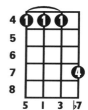
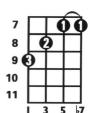

## Bm7
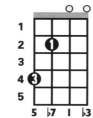
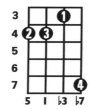
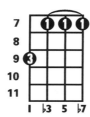

## B5
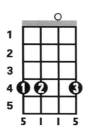
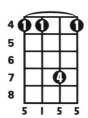
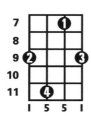

## B6
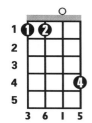
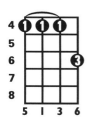
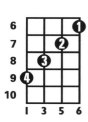

## Bm6
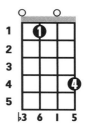
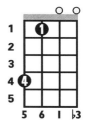
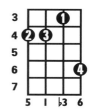

## Bmaj7
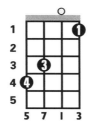
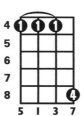
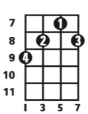

67

# B Chords

## B°

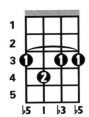

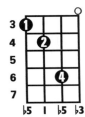

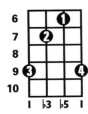

## B°7

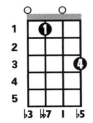

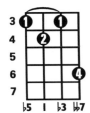

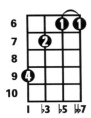

## B-5

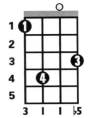

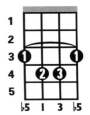

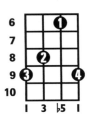

## B+

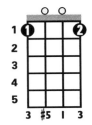

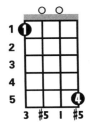

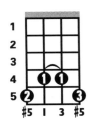

## Bsus2

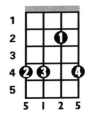

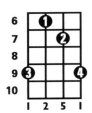

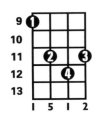

## Bsus4

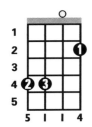

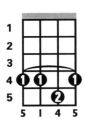

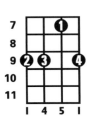

## B7sus4

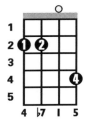

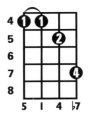

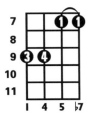

## Bm7-5

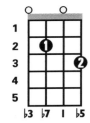

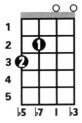

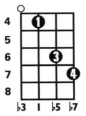

## Badd9

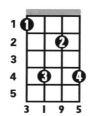

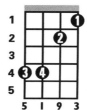

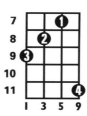

## Bmadd9

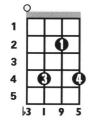

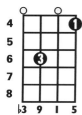

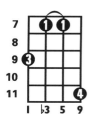

## B6add9

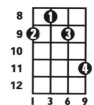

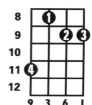

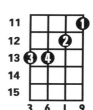

## Bm6add9

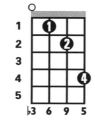

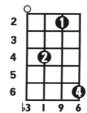

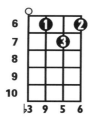

## B7-5

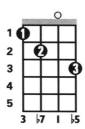

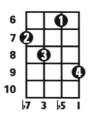

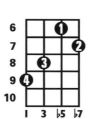

## B7+5

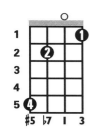

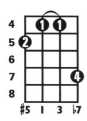

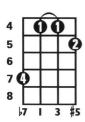

## B7-9

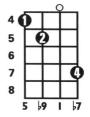

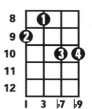

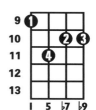

## B7+9

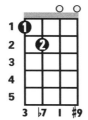

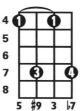

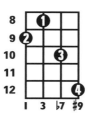

# B Chords

### Bm(maj7)
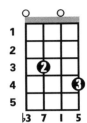
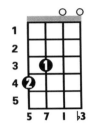
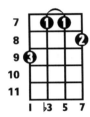

### Bmaj7-5
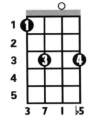
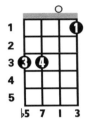
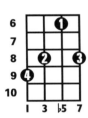

### Bmaj7+5
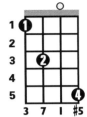
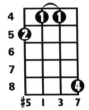
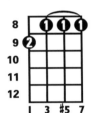

### B9
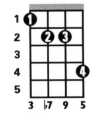
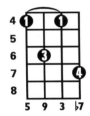
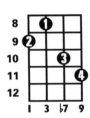

### Bm9
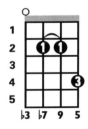
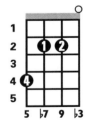
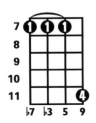

### Bmaj9
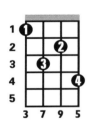
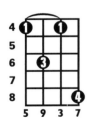
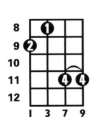

### B11
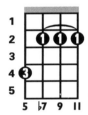
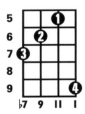
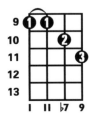

### B13
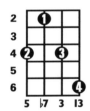
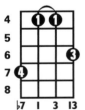
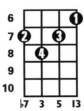

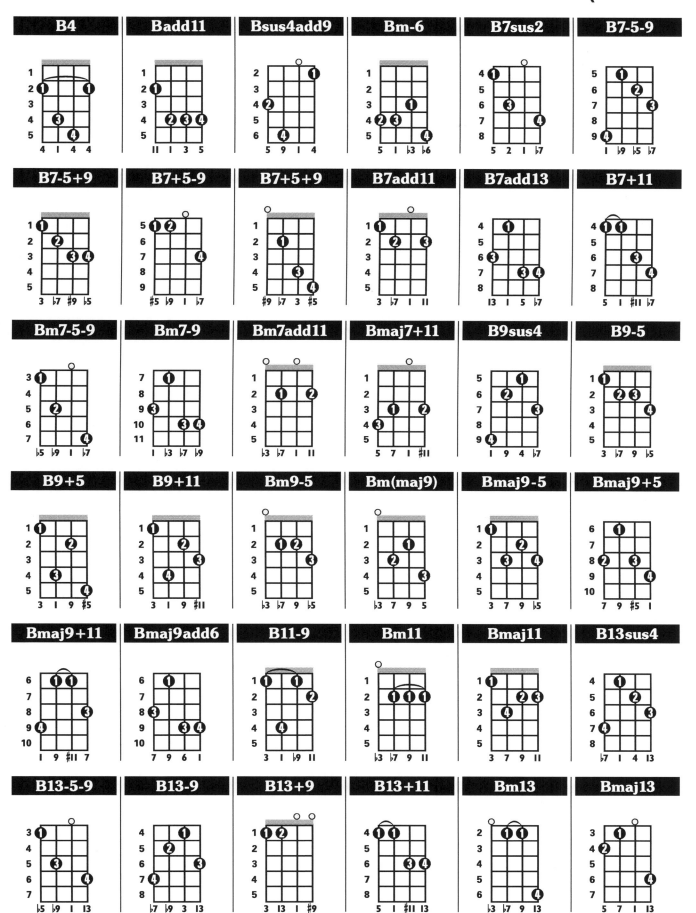

# Major Slash Chords

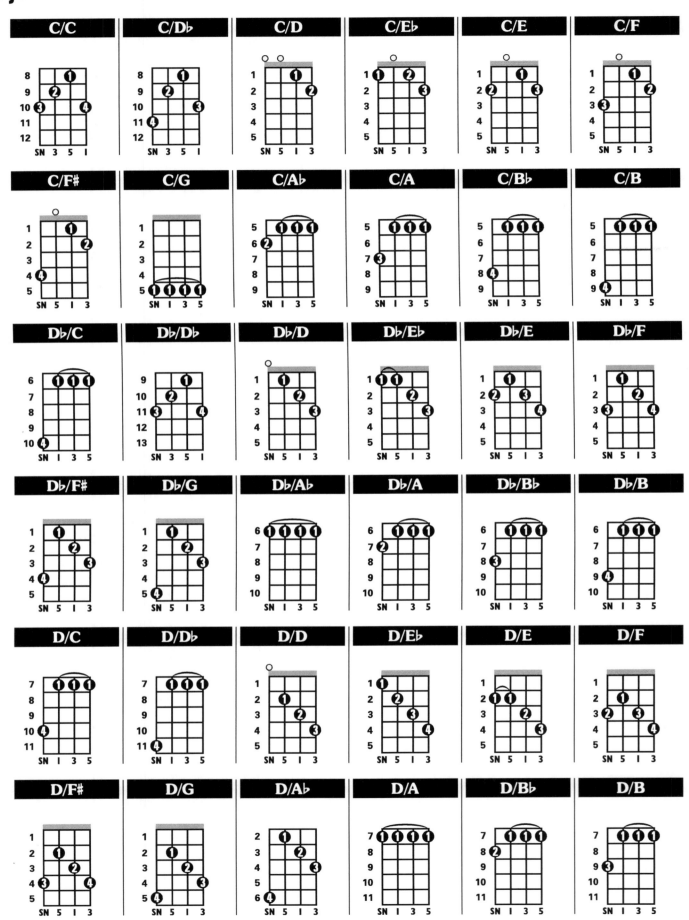

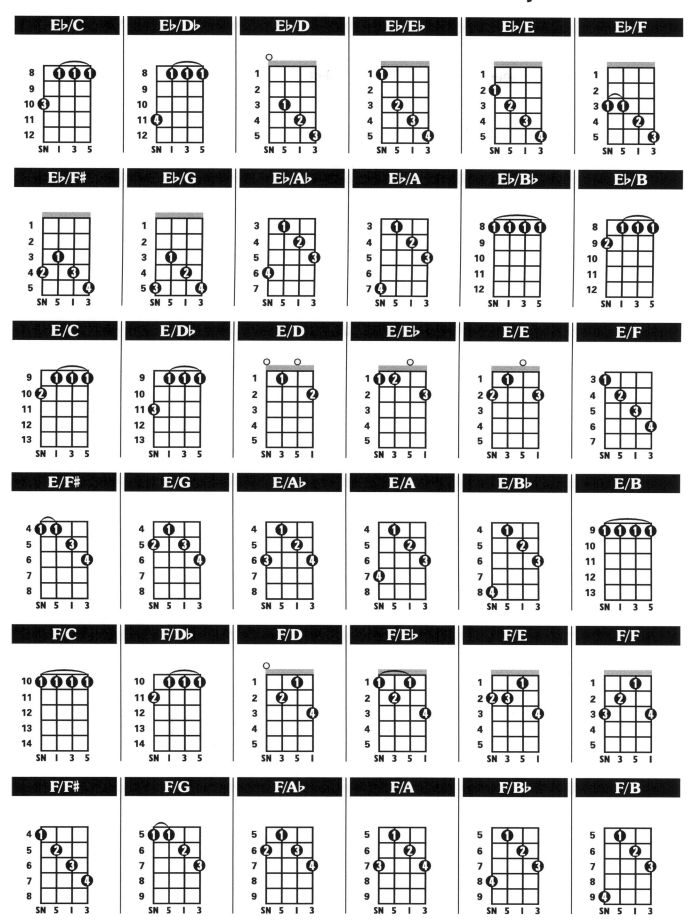

# Major Slash Chords

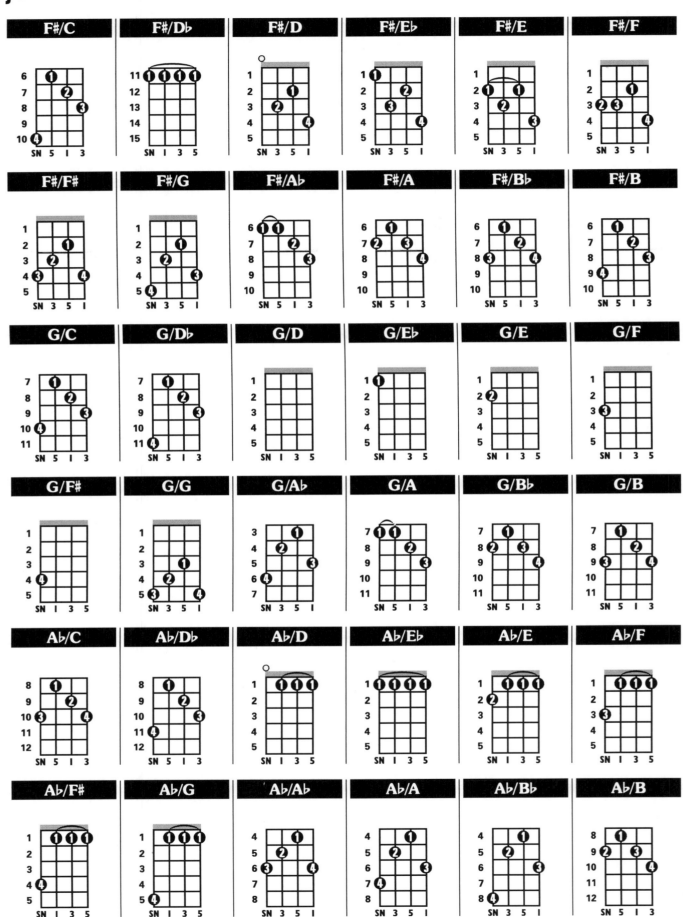

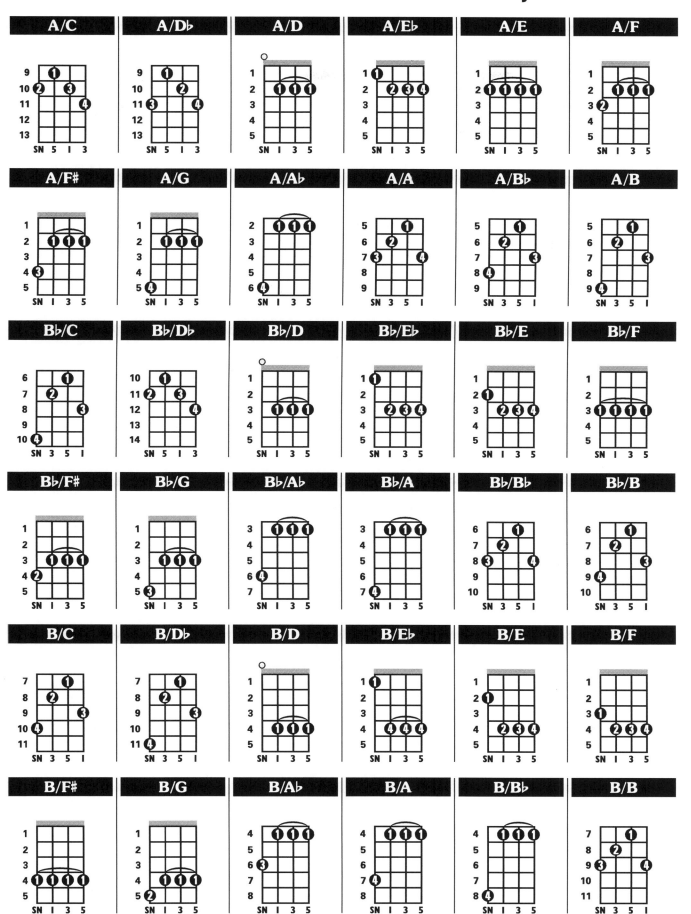

# A Selection of Moveable Chord Shapes

## Major

| Fret | Note |
|---|---|
| 1 | C#/Db |
| 2 | D |
| 3 | D#/Eb |
| 4 | E |
| 5 | F |
| 6 | F#/Gb |
| 7 | G |
| 8 | G#/Ab |
| 9 | A |
| 10 | A#/Bb |
| 11 | B |
| 12 | C |

3 5 1 3

## Major

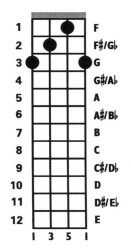

## Major

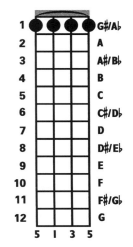

## Major

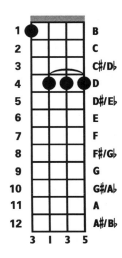

## Minor

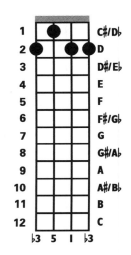

## Minor

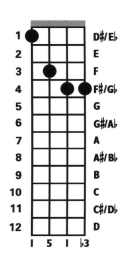

## Minor

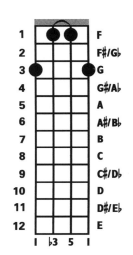

## Minor

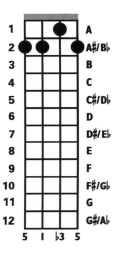

## Seventh

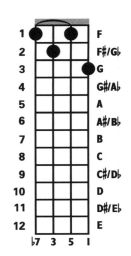

## Seventh

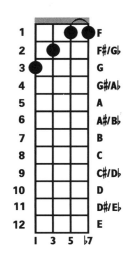

## Seventh

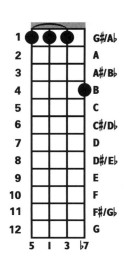

## Seventh

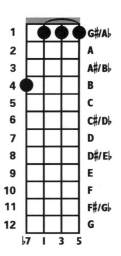

# A Selection of Moveable Chord Shapes

## Minor Seventh
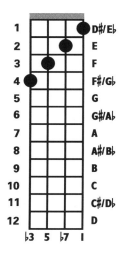

| | |
|---|---|
| 1 | D#/Eb |
| 2 | E |
| 3 | F |
| 4 | F#/Gb |
| 5 | G |
| 6 | G#/Ab |
| 7 | A |
| 8 | A#/Bb |
| 9 | B |
| 10 | C |
| 11 | C#/Db |
| 12 | D |

I  5  b7  b3

## Minor Seventh
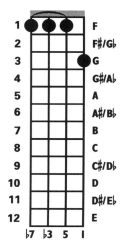

| | |
|---|---|
| 1 | D#/Eb |
| 2 | E |
| 3 | F |
| 4 | F#/Gb |
| 5 | G |
| 6 | G#/Ab |
| 7 | A |
| 8 | A#/Bb |
| 9 | B |
| 10 | C |
| 11 | C#/Db |
| 12 | D |

b3  5  b7  I

## Minor Seventh
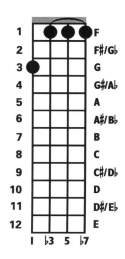

| | |
|---|---|
| 1 | F |
| 2 | F#/Gb |
| 3 | G |
| 4 | G#/Ab |
| 5 | A |
| 6 | A#/Bb |
| 7 | B |
| 8 | C |
| 9 | C#/Db |
| 10 | D |
| 11 | D#/Eb |
| 12 | E |

b7  b3  5  I

## Minor Seventh

| | |
|---|---|
| 1 | F |
| 2 | F#/Gb |
| 3 | G |
| 4 | G#/Ab |
| 5 | A |
| 6 | A#/Bb |
| 7 | B |
| 8 | C |
| 9 | C#/Db |
| 10 | D |
| 11 | D#/Eb |
| 12 | E |

I  b3  5  b7

## Sixth
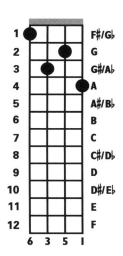

| | |
|---|---|
| 1 | F#/Gb |
| 2 | G |
| 3 | G#/Ab |
| 4 | A |
| 5 | A#/Bb |
| 6 | B |
| 7 | C |
| 8 | C#/Db |
| 9 | D |
| 10 | D#/Eb |
| 11 | E |
| 12 | F |

6  3  5  I

## Sixth
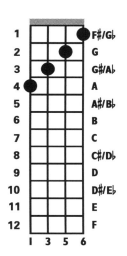

| | |
|---|---|
| 1 | F#/Gb |
| 2 | G |
| 3 | G#/Ab |
| 4 | A |
| 5 | A#/Bb |
| 6 | B |
| 7 | C |
| 8 | C#/Db |
| 9 | D |
| 10 | D#/Eb |
| 11 | E |
| 12 | F |

I  3  5  6

## Sixth
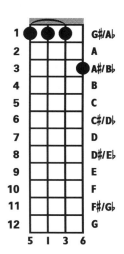

| | |
|---|---|
| 1 | G#/Ab |
| 2 | A |
| 3 | A#/Bb |
| 4 | B |
| 5 | C |
| 6 | C#/Db |
| 7 | D |
| 8 | D#/Eb |
| 9 | E |
| 10 | F |
| 11 | F#/Gb |
| 12 | G |

5  I  3  6

## Sixth
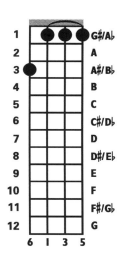

| | |
|---|---|
| 1 | G#/Ab |
| 2 | A |
| 3 | A#/Bb |
| 4 | B |
| 5 | C |
| 6 | C#/Db |
| 7 | D |
| 8 | D#/Eb |
| 9 | E |
| 10 | F |
| 11 | F#/Gb |
| 12 | G |

6  I  3  5

## Minor Sixth
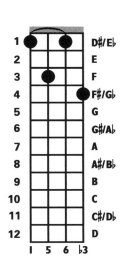

| | |
|---|---|
| 1 | D#/Eb |
| 2 | E |
| 3 | F |
| 4 | F#/Gb |
| 5 | G |
| 6 | G#/Ab |
| 7 | A |
| 8 | A#/Bb |
| 9 | B |
| 10 | C |
| 11 | C#/Db |
| 12 | D |

I  5  6  b3

## Minor Sixth
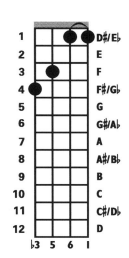

| | |
|---|---|
| 1 | D#/Eb |
| 2 | E |
| 3 | F |
| 4 | F#/Gb |
| 5 | G |
| 6 | G#/Ab |
| 7 | A |
| 8 | A#/Bb |
| 9 | B |
| 10 | C |
| 11 | C#/Db |
| 12 | D |

b3  5  6  I

## Minor Sixth
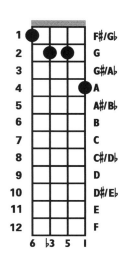

| | |
|---|---|
| 1 | F#/Gb |
| 2 | G |
| 3 | G#/Ab |
| 4 | A |
| 5 | A#/Bb |
| 6 | B |
| 7 | C |
| 8 | C#/Db |
| 9 | D |
| 10 | D#/Eb |
| 11 | E |
| 12 | F |

6  b3  5  I

## Minor Sixth
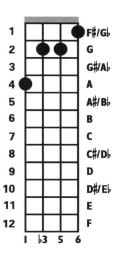

| | |
|---|---|
| 1 | F#/Gb |
| 2 | G |
| 3 | G#/Ab |
| 4 | A |
| 5 | A#/Bb |
| 6 | B |
| 7 | C |
| 8 | C#/Db |
| 9 | D |
| 10 | D#/Eb |
| 11 | E |
| 12 | F |

I  b3  5  6

# A Selection of Moveable Chord Shapes

## Major Seventh

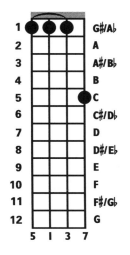

1 — F
2 — F#/Gb
3 — G
4 — G#/Ab
5 — A
6 — A#/Bb
7 — B
8 — C
9 — C#/Db
10 — D
11 — D#/Eb
12 — E

1  3  5  7

## Major Seventh

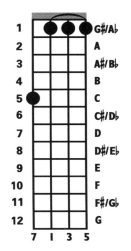

1 — G#/Ab
2 — A
3 — A#/Bb
4 — B
5 — C
6 — C#/Db
7 — D
8 — D#/Eb
9 — E
10 — F
11 — F#/Gb
12 — G

5  1  3  7

## Major Seventh

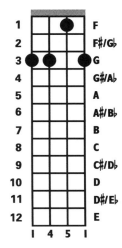

1 — G#/Ab
2 — A
3 — A#/Bb
4 — B
5 — C
6 — C#/Db
7 — D
8 — D#/Eb
9 — E
10 — F
11 — F#/Gb
12 — G

7  1  3  5

## Suspended Fourth

1 — F
2 — F#/Gb
3 — G
4 — G#/Ab
5 — A
6 — A#/Bb
7 — B
8 — C
9 — C#/Db
10 — D
11 — D#/Eb
12 — E

1  4  5  1

## Suspended Fourth

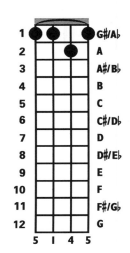

1 — G#/Ab
2 — A
3 — A#/Bb
4 — B
5 — C
6 — C#/Db
7 — D
8 — D#/Eb
9 — E
10 — F
11 — F#/Gb
12 — G

5  1  4  5

## Suspended Fourth

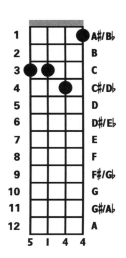

1 — A#/Bb
2 — B
3 — C
4 — C#/Db
5 — D
6 — D#/Eb
7 — E
8 — F
9 — F#/Gb
10 — G
11 — G#/Ab
12 — A

5  1  4  4

## Diminished

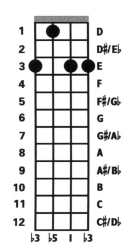

1 — D
2 — D#/Eb
3 — E
4 — F
5 — F#/Gb
6 — G
7 — G#/Ab
8 — A
9 — A#/Bb
10 — B
11 — C
12 — C#/Db

b3  b5  1  b3

## Diminished

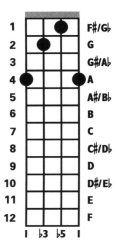

1 — F#/Gb
2 — G
3 — G#/Ab
4 — A
5 — A#/Bb
6 — B
7 — C
8 — C#/Db
9 — D
10 — D#/Eb
11 — E
12 — F

1  b3  b5  1

## Diminished

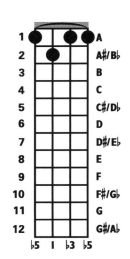

1 — A
2 — A#/Bb
3 — B
4 — C
5 — C#/Db
6 — D
7 — D#/Eb
8 — E
9 — F
10 — F#/Gb
11 — G
12 — G#/Ab

b5  1  b3  b5

## Augmented

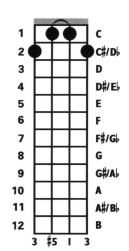

1 — C
2 — C#/Db
3 — D
4 — D#/Eb
5 — E
6 — F
7 — F#/Gb
8 — G
9 — G#/Ab
10 — A
11 — A#/Bb
12 — B

3  #5  1  3

## Augmented

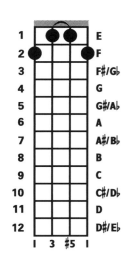

1 — E
2 — F
3 — F#/Gb
4 — G
5 — G#/Ab
6 — A
7 — A#/Bb
8 — B
9 — C
10 — C#/Db
11 — D
12 — D#/Eb

1  3  #5  1

## Augmented

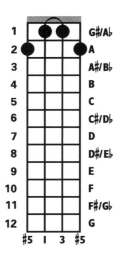

1 — G#/Ab
2 — A
3 — A#/Bb
4 — B
5 — C
6 — C#/Db
7 — D
8 — D#/Eb
9 — E
10 — F
11 — F#/Gb
12 — G

#5  1  3  #5

# A Selection of Moveable Chord Shapes

### Diminished Seventh
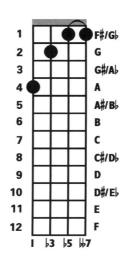

| | |
|---|---|
| 1 | F#/Gb |
| 2 | G |
| 3 | G#/Ab |
| 4 | A |
| 5 | A#/Bb |
| 6 | B |
| 7 | C |
| 8 | C#/Db |
| 9 | D |
| 10 | D#/Eb |
| 11 | E |
| 12 | F |

I  b3  b5  b7

### Diminished Seventh
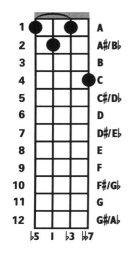

| | |
|---|---|
| 1 | A |
| 2 | A#/Bb |
| 3 | B |
| 4 | C |
| 5 | C#/Db |
| 6 | D |
| 7 | D#/Eb |
| 8 | E |
| 9 | F |
| 10 | F#/Gb |
| 11 | G |
| 12 | G#/Ab |

b5  I  b3  b7

### Fifth
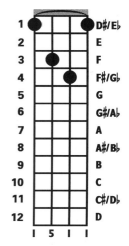

| | |
|---|---|
| 1 | D#/Eb |
| 2 | E |
| 3 | F |
| 4 | F#/Gb |
| 5 | G |
| 6 | G#/Ab |
| 7 | A |
| 8 | A#/Bb |
| 9 | B |
| 10 | C |
| 11 | C#/Db |
| 12 | D |

I  5  I  I

### Fifth
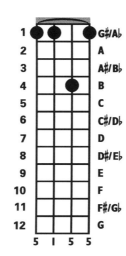

| | |
|---|---|
| 1 | G#/Ab |
| 2 | A |
| 3 | A#/Bb |
| 4 | B |
| 5 | C |
| 6 | C#/Db |
| 7 | D |
| 8 | D#/Eb |
| 9 | E |
| 10 | F |
| 11 | F#/Gb |
| 12 | G |

5  I  5  5

### Seventh Suspended
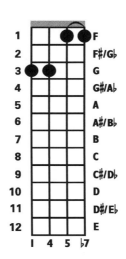

| | |
|---|---|
| 1 | F |
| 2 | F#/Gb |
| 3 | G |
| 4 | G#/Ab |
| 5 | A |
| 6 | A#/Bb |
| 7 | B |
| 8 | C |
| 9 | C#/Db |
| 10 | D |
| 11 | D#/Eb |
| 12 | E |

I  4  5  b7

### Added Ninth
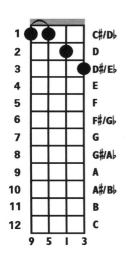

| | |
|---|---|
| 1 | C#/Db |
| 2 | D |
| 3 | D#/Eb |
| 4 | E |
| 5 | F |
| 6 | F#/Gb |
| 7 | G |
| 8 | G#/Ab |
| 9 | A |
| 10 | A#/Bb |
| 11 | B |
| 12 | C |

9  5  I  3

### Added Ninth
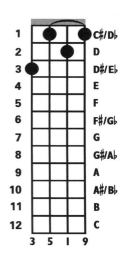

| | |
|---|---|
| 1 | C#/Db |
| 2 | D |
| 3 | D#/Eb |
| 4 | E |
| 5 | F |
| 6 | F#/Gb |
| 7 | G |
| 8 | G#/Ab |
| 9 | A |
| 10 | A#/Bb |
| 11 | B |
| 12 | C |

3  5  I  9

### Ninth
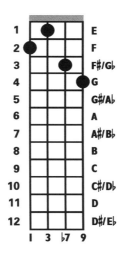

| | |
|---|---|
| 1 | E |
| 2 | F |
| 3 | F#/Gb |
| 4 | G |
| 5 | G#/Ab |
| 6 | A |
| 7 | A#/Bb |
| 8 | B |
| 9 | C |
| 10 | C#/Db |
| 11 | D |
| 12 | D#/Eb |

I  3  b7  9

### Minor Ninth
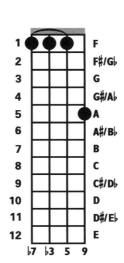

| | |
|---|---|
| 1 | F |
| 2 | F#/Gb |
| 3 | G |
| 4 | G#/Ab |
| 5 | A |
| 6 | A#/Bb |
| 7 | B |
| 8 | C |
| 9 | C#/Db |
| 10 | D |
| 11 | D#/Eb |
| 12 | E |

b7  b3  5  9

### Major Ninth
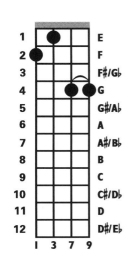

| | |
|---|---|
| 1 | E |
| 2 | F |
| 3 | F#/Gb |
| 4 | G |
| 5 | G#/Ab |
| 6 | A |
| 7 | A#/Bb |
| 8 | B |
| 9 | C |
| 10 | C#/Db |
| 11 | D |
| 12 | D#/Eb |

I  3  7  9

### Eleventh
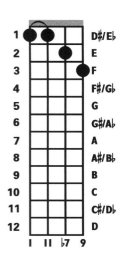

| | |
|---|---|
| 1 | D#/Eb |
| 2 | E |
| 3 | F |
| 4 | F#/Gb |
| 5 | G |
| 6 | G#/Ab |
| 7 | A |
| 8 | A#/Bb |
| 9 | B |
| 10 | C |
| 11 | C#/Db |
| 12 | D |

I  II  b7  9

### Thirteenth
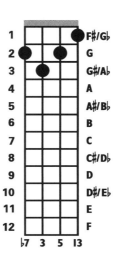

| | |
|---|---|
| 1 | F#/Gb |
| 2 | G |
| 3 | G#/Ab |
| 4 | A |
| 5 | A#/Bb |
| 6 | B |
| 7 | C |
| 8 | C#/Db |
| 9 | D |
| 10 | D#/Eb |
| 11 | E |
| 12 | F |

b7  3  5  I3

# UKULELE FAMILY FACTFILE

### Akulele

A new design of ukulele carved from a single piece of wood, much like the construction of the Andean charango. The Akulele comes in a variety of configurations including a taropatch model and a higher pitched sopranino, which has a shorter scale than the soprano and is tuned a fifth higher (D-G-B-E). With it's origins coming out of the marriage between ukulele and charango, the sopranino could be compared to the relationship between the charango and its little sibling, the walaycho.

### Baritone Ukulele

The big brother of the ukulele family first appeared in 1940s America, many decades after it's soprano forebear. The idea behind the baritone uke was said to have been thought up by U.S. variety show host and ukelele player, Arthur Godfrey, a major star at the birth of popular television. Although it could be argued, the baritone is more like a four stringed guitar than a traditional uke, its remained a popular minority instrument ever since it's inception. The baritone uke is tuned to an open G6 chord (D-G-B-E), a fourth lower than standard ukulele C6 tuning.

### Braguinha

A Madeiran instrument said to have been the main ancestor of today's ukulele. The Braguinha features the same scale length as a standard soprano uke, but is tuned roughly a fourth lower to an open G major chord (D-G-B-D). The name of the instrument itself is taken from the Madeiran city of Braga.

### Cavaquinho

The cavaquinho is probably best known for its role in Brazilian samba and choro music, where it's played with a pick, using a rhythmical strumming technique. Standard tuning is generally considered to be based on a G major open chord (D-G-B-D). Other popular tunings include G-G-B-D (again, another inversion of the open G major) and A-A-C#-E (open A major chord). D-G-B-E is also used, particularly by guitarists. This tuning is shared with the baritone uke. Apart from Brazil, this little uke-sized instrument can be found in Madeira, The Azores, Cape Verde, Hawaii and other locations where Portguese immigration has had a sizeable impact.

### Charango

Although the charango isn't strictly a member of the ukulele family, it shares many attributes with its Hawaiian cousin, including re-entrant tuning, plus an additional high course (G-C-E-A-E). Again, like the soprano uke, it's tuned to an open C6 chord, but features double nylon courses of strings instead of singles. The original charangos were made from the shells of the poor unfortunate armadillo or *quirquincho*. Fortunately, today this practice is dying out, with most instrument bodies being constructed from indigenous woods from the Andean region of South America. The body shape of the charango also differs from the uke, featuring a rounded back, reflecting its armadillo shell ancestry.

The charango, much like the ukulele is also part of a larger family group. The charango is pitched in the soprano range, while the ronroco (or *ronrroco*) is a full octave lower, the charangon a fourth or a fifth lower and the walaycho (*hualaycho, waylacho* or *maulincho*), a fourth or a fifth higher. All generally feature nylon strings, except the walaycho which sometimes utilizes steel strings.

### Concert Ukulele

The first concert ukulele appeared in 1925 as a result of the Martin guitar company failing to sell sufficient quantities of its 8-string taropatch model. The solution was a simple one. The double courses were removed and the larger bodied concert uke was born. Today the concert model slots in between the soprano and tenor models in terms of size. The tuning is identical to the soprano.

### Guitarlele

Arguably, the guitarlele can be viewed as a scaled down guitar, rather than a true member of the ukulele family. The physical size is around that of the baritone uke, but with a wider fretboard to accommodate the two additional lower strings. The tuning is identical to a regular guitar (E-A-D-G-B-E).

### Rajão

The 5-string rajão, like it's sister instrument, the braguinha, originates in the Portuguese island of Madeira where it's used mainly for rhythm accompaniment. The D-G-C-E-A tuning is re-entrant like the soprano ukulele, except it employs this configuration on both the 4th and 5th strings.

### Re-entrant Tuning

Best exemplified by the aide-mémoire *"my dog has fleas"*, representing the 4 strings of the ukulele from 4th to 1st. A re-entrant arrangement refers to a tuning that doesn't follow a strict high to low or low to high succession. In the case of the soprano uke, the 3rd string is the lowest sounding, rather than 4th. The tenor and baritone models don't generally employ re-entrant tuning. The rajão, the predecessor to the uke, also features re-entrant tuning.

### Soprano Ukulele

The origins of the ukulele began in 1879, when a German ship, the Ravenscrag, carried three cabinet makers, Manuel Nunes, Augusto Dias and Jose de Espirito Santo, to the Hawaiian islands to provide much needed cabinet making skills for the existing Madeiran emigrees. Although today we think of luthery and cabinet making as separate skills, it wasn't uncommon in previous centuries for a cabinet maker to double up his craft and maximize earnings by combining the two disciplines. So Nunes, possibly aided by Dias and Santo, came up with a design based on the body shape of the braguinha and the re-entrant tuning of the rajão, albeit with four strings instead of five.

The ukulele soon gained a foothold in Hawaiian life and culture, even finding its way into the hands of King David Kalaukea, a talented musician in his own right. Because the tuning was essentially a transposed four string guitar, people were immediately able to adjust to the new instrument. It wasn't long before this musical hybrid became a cultural icon and a tourist memento for anybody visiting the islands. Unlike other instruments whose popularity has waxed and waned over the years, the little uke has managed to stave off passing trends and remains a popular purchase for both young and old. According to historians, its greatest period of popularity lay between 1915-1935, when it became the number one musical instrument in the average American family home. It's unlikely since the emergence of the guitar in its many guises, that the little uke will rise to such dizzy heights again. But because of it's portability, relatively low starting price and ease of playing, it will always maintain a healthy niche position in the instrument market.

The name ukulele is officially thought to translate from the Hawaiian, as *jumping flea*. But another possible origin could lie in the words *ukeki*, a type of plucked Hawaiian jew's harp and *mele*, the local word for song.

Most quality instruments are generally constructed from the local koa wood, but you'll find makers using anything from plywood to cardboard to produce this little relative of the guitar. The tonal qualities of the latter, as you can imagine, are open to question!

Although we refer to the standard ukulele design today as the soprano, this prefix was added later to differentiate between the four family members. Standard tuning for most soprano ukes is GCEA (or an open C6 chord). ADF#B (open D6) was also used earlier in the 20th century for greater sound projection and is still popular with a minority of players today.

### Taropatch

The taropatch is an 8-string variant of the ukulele divided up into 4 double courses. Its origins lie with the rajão after native Hawaiians adopted the ukulele, but wanted a bigger overall sound. An additional course was added to each string and the result was the taropatch *'fiddle'* as it came to be known.

## Tenor Ukulele

The second largest of the ukulele family. The tenor differs from the soprano and concert models in its use of guitar-style high to low stringing, rather than the re-entrant configuration found on traditional ukes. The most popular tuning for the tenor is identical to the soprano and concert models, G-C-E-A, but D-G-B-E has also gained favour with many musicians over the years, including famous uke players like Lyle Ritz.

## Timple

A close relative of the ukulele originating in the Canary Islands and Murcia, the timple (pronounced *teem-play*) has an additional fifth string and a distinctive rounded back. The tuning is generally A-D-F#-B-E (from low to high). Basically, a traditional ukulele D6 tuning with an additional high E string. 4-string versions also exist. The timple is thought to have Berber origins.

## Tiple

Unlike its Hawaiian relative, the tiple in its many incarnations, is generally strung with steel strings which are arranged in triple and double courses. The version familiar to American and Western musicians was designed by *C.F. Martin & Company*, better known for their prowess in acoustic guitar design. The *Martin* tiple is usually tuned A-D-F#-B with the middle two courses tripled and the two outer courses doubled.

Other types of tiple include:
Banjo Tiple (Peru): *A little banjo with 4 double courses of strings.*
Colombian Tiple: *12-string guitar-like instrument divided up into 4 triple stringed courses*
Marxochime Hawaiian Tiple: *A zither-lap steel guitar hybrid tiple.*
Spanish Tiple (Spain): *A little guitar style tiple from Menorca.*
Tiple Argentino (Argentina): *Little guitar-style instrument with 6 strings.*
Tiple Cubano (Cuba): *Cuban instrument with either 5 single string or 5 double courses (like the taropatch or charango).*
Tiple Doliente (Puerto Rico): *A popular five stringed instrument.*
Tiple Dominicano (Dominican Republic): *5 double coursed bandurria-like instrument*
Tiple Grande de Ponce (Puerto Rico): *A narrow waisted, larger member of the tiple group.*
Tiple Peruano (Peru): *Peruvian tiple with 4 single or double strings.*
Tiple Requinto Costanero (Puerto Rico): *Small version of the tiplón.*
Tiple Requinto de la Montaña (Puerto Rico): *Small 3-stringed version of the doliente.*
Tiple Uruguayo (Uruguay): *A little guitar-style of tiple with 6 strings.*
Tiple Venezolano (Venezuela): *Smaller version of the Colombian tiple, featuring 4 triple string courses.*
Tiplón *or* Tiple con Macho (Puerto Rico): *The largest family member with a 5th tuning peg much like the 5-string banjo.*

The word *tiple* (pronounced *tee-play*) translated from the Spanish, means treble or soprano.

## Ukelele

Alternative spelling of ukulele.

## Ukulele-Banjo, Banjo-Ukulele *or* Banjolele

A popular instrument with its heyday in the 20's and 30's, the banjolele or banjo-uke is basically a ukulele in a short scaled banjo's body. These entertaining instruments can be tuned GCEA or ADF#B. The banjolele was popularized in the U.K. by comedian *George Formby*, where the instrument was mistakenly referred to at the time as a ukulele. The name banjolele was originally created by the *Keech Brothers, Alvin* and *Kel*.

## Venezuelan Cuatro

The South American cuatro's history can be traced back to its long defunct ancestor, the 4-string Spanish guitar. Again, like several of the instruments in this family group, the cuatro is tuned to the same fundamental intervals as the first four strings of a classical guitar - in this case A-D-F#-B, like the soprano uke's D6 tuning. Where it differs is in the positioning of the re-entrant strings. With the ukulele and rajão, the higher strings can be found on the 4th and 5th strings. With the cuatro, the 2nd and 3rd strings are re-entrant (namely the D and F#). Although most musicians use this tuning, an alternative was created by reknowned cuatro player, Fredy Reyna in 1948. Rebelling against the re-entrant standard, Reyna re-strung the cuatro to a more recognizable low to high tuning (E-A-C#-F#), but still retained the relationship, based on guitar tuning (transposed into the key of A6).

Very much akin to the English language aide-mémoire *"my dog has fleas"*, the cuatro's tuning can be remembered by singing the following two words, *"Cam-bur pin-tón"*, or ripe banana!

The 4-string or Venezuelan cuatro is not to be confused with the Puerto Rican cuatro which illogically has 10 steel strings in 5 double courses. The design bares little or no resemblance to the more guitar-like mainland instrument (the tuning is B-E-A-D-G). The shape is very reminiscent of a member of the violin family with it's instantly recognizable sculpted waist and upper/lower bouts.

## Ukulele Family Instrument Tunings

| | |
|---|---|
| Baritone Ukulele Standard Tuning | DGBE (G6) |
| Concert Ukulele Standard Tuning | GCEA (C6) |
| Concert Ukulele Alternative Tuning | ADF#B (D6) |
| Soprano Akulele Standard Tuning | GCEA (C6) |
| Soprano Ukulele Standard Tuning | GCEA (C6) |
| Soprano Ukulele Alternative Tuning | ADF#B (D6) |
| Sopranino Akulele Standard Tuning | DGBE (G6) |
| Taropatch Standard Tuning | GCEA (C6) |
| Tenor Ukulele Standard Tuning | GCEA (C6) |
| Tenor Ukulele Alternative Tuning | DGBE (G6) |
| Ukulele-Banjo Standard Tuning | GCEA (C6) |
| Ukulele-Banjo Alternative Tuning | ADF#B (D6) |

## Related Instrument Tunings

| | |
|---|---|
| Braguinha Standard Tuning | DGBD (G Major) |
| Cavaquinho Standard Tuning | DGBD (G Major) |
| Cavaquinho Alternative tuning | GGBD (G Major) |
| Cavaquinho Alternative Tuning | AAC#E (A Major) |
| Cavaquinho Guitar Tuning | DGBE (G6) |
| Charango Standard Tuning | GCEAE (C6) |
| Charangon Standard Tuning 1 | CFADA (F6) |
| Charangon Standard Tuning 2 | DGBEB (G6) |
| Guitarlele Standard Tuning | EADGBE (G6/9) |
| Martin Tiple Standard Tuning | ADF#B (D6) |
| Rajão Standard Tuning | DGCEA (C6/9) |
| Ronroco Standard Tuning | GCEAE (G6) |
| Timple Canario Standard Tuning | ADF#BE (D6/9) |
| Venezuelan Cuatro Standard Tuning | ADF#B (D6) |
| Venezuelan Cuatro F. Reyna Tuning | EAC#F# (A6) |
| Walaycho Standard Tuning 1 | CFADA (F6) |
| Walaycho Standard Tuning 2 | DGBEB (G6) |

# ALTERNATIVE CHORD NAMES

| | |
|---|---|
| C | **CM** *or* **Cmaj** |
| Cm | **Cmin** *or* **C-** |
| C-5 | **C-5 or C(♭5)** |
| C° | **Cdim** |
| C4 | **Csus4(no 5th)** *or* **Csus(no 5th)** |
| C5 | **C Power Chord** *or* **C(no 3rd)** |
| Csus2 | **C(sus2)** *or* **C2** |
| Csus4 | **Csus** *or* **C(sus4)** |
| Csus4add9 | **Csus(add9)** |
| C+ | **Caug, C+5** *or* **C(♯5)** |
| C6 | **CM6** *or* **CMaj6** |
| Cadd9 | **Cadd2** |
| Cm6 | **C-6** *or* **Cmin6** |
| Cmadd9 | **Cmadd2** *or* **C-(add9)** |
| C6add9 | **C6/9, C⁶₉** *or* **CMaj6(add9)** |
| Cm6add9 | **Cm6/9** *or* **Cm⁶₉** |
| C°7 | **Cdim7** |
| C7 | **Cdom** |
| C7sus2 | **C7(sus2)** |
| C7sus4 | **C7sus, C7(sus4)** *or* **Csus11** |
| C7-5 | **C7♭5** |
| C7+5 | **C7+** *or* **C7♯5** |
| C7-9 | **C7♭9** *or* **C7(add♭9)** |
| C7+9 | **C7♯9** *or* **C7(add♯9)** |
| C7-5-9 | **C7♭5♭9** |
| C7+5-9 | **C7♯5♭9** |
| C7+5+9 | **C7♯5♯9** |
| C7add11 | **C7/11** *or* **C⁷₁₁** |
| C7+11 | **C7♯11** |
| Cm7 | **C-7, Cmi7** *or* **Cmin7** |
| Cm7-5 | **Cm7♭5, C-7-5** *or* **Cᵒ̸** |
| Cm7-5-9 | **Cm7♭5♭9** |
| Cm7-9 | **Cm7♭9** |
| Cm7add11 | **Cm** |
| Cm(maj7) | **Cm♯7, CM7-5, CmM7** *or* **C-△** |
| Cmaj7 | **CM7** *or* **C△(Delta)** |
| Cmaj7-5 | **CM7-5, C△♭5** *or* **Cmaj7♭5** |
| Cmaj7+5 | **CM7+5, C△5+** *or* **Cmaj7♯11** |
| Cmaj7+11 | **CM7+11, C△+♯11** *or* **Cmaj7♯11** |
| C9 | **C7(add9)** |
| C9sus4 | **C9sus** *or* **C9(sus4)** |
| C9-5 | **C9♭5** |
| C9+5 | **C9♯5** |
| C9+11 | **C9♯11** |
| Cm9 | **C-9** *or* **Cmin9** |
| Cm9-5 | **Cm9♭5** |
| Cm(maj9) | **Cm9(maj7), CmM9** *or* **Cm(addM9)** |
| Cmaj9 | **CM9, Cmaj7(add9), C△9** *or* **CM7(add9)** |
| Cmaj9-5 | **CM9-5, Cmaj9♭5, C△9♭5** *or* **CM9♭5** |
| Cmaj9+5 | **CM9+5, Cmaj9♯5, C△9♯5** |
| Cmaj9add6 | **CM9add6** *or* **C△9add6** |
| Cmaj9+11 | **CM9+11, Cmaj9♯11, C△9♯11** *or* **CM9♯11** |
| C11 | **C7(add11)** |
| C11-9 | **C11♭9** |
| Cm11 | **C-11** *or* **Cmin11** |
| Cmaj11 | **CM11, Cmaj7(add11), C△11, CM7(add11)** |
| C13 | **C7/6(no 9th)** *or* **C7(add13)** |
| C13sus4 | **C13sus** *or* **C13(sus4)** |
| C13-5-9 | **C13♭5♭9** |
| C13-9 | **C13♭9** |
| C13+9 | **C13♯9** |
| C13+11 | **C13♯11** *or* **C13aug11** |

| | |
|---|---|
| Cm13 | **C-13** *or* **Cmin13** |
| Cmaj13 | **CM13, Cmaj7(add13), C△13** *or* **CM7(add13)** |

| | |
|---|---|
| M | **major** |
| m | **minor** |
| - | **minor** |
| dim | **diminished** |
| ° | **diminished** |
| ∅ | **half diminished** |
| sus | **suspended** |
| aug | **augmented** |
| + | **augmented** |
| add | **added** |
| dom | **dominant** |
| △ | **delta /major seventh** |
| Q(3) | **quartal / double fourth** |
| ♯ | **sharp** |
| ✕ | **double sharp** |
| ♭ | **flat** |
| ♭♭ | **double flat** |

| | |
|---|---|
| Do | **Spanish for C** |
| Dó | **Portuguese for C** |
| Re | **Spanish for D** |
| Ré | **Portuguese for D** |
| Mi | **Spanish & Portuguese for E** |
| Fa | **Spanish & Portuguese for F** |
| So | **Spanish for G** |
| Sol | **Portuguese for G** |
| La | **Spanish for A** |
| Lá | **Portuguese for A** |
| Si | **Spanish & Portuguese for B** |
| H | **German for B** |

## English Tonic Sol-fa

| | |
|---|---|
| Do | **C** |
| Re | **D** |
| Me | **E** |
| Fa | **F** |
| Sol | **G** |
| La | **A** |
| Ti | **B** |

The majority of music books will use the chords featured in the first column (on the far left and top right), but should you come across alternatives, consult this guide for other naming conventions.

The list above includes most of the symbols and abbreviations that you're likely to encounter in the majority of music books.

# NOTES

# NOTES

# NOTES

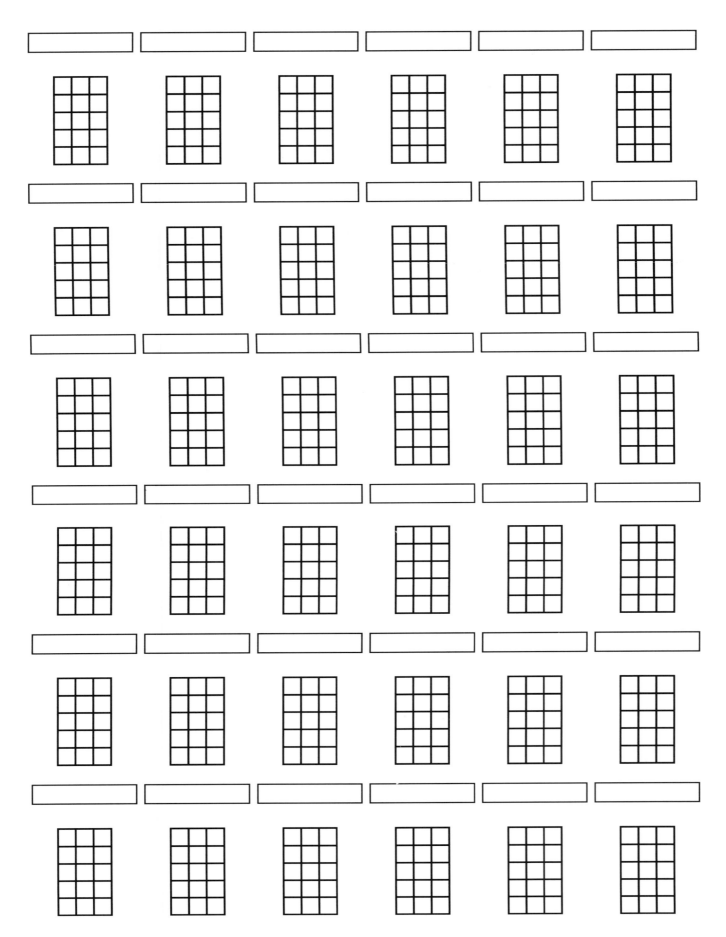

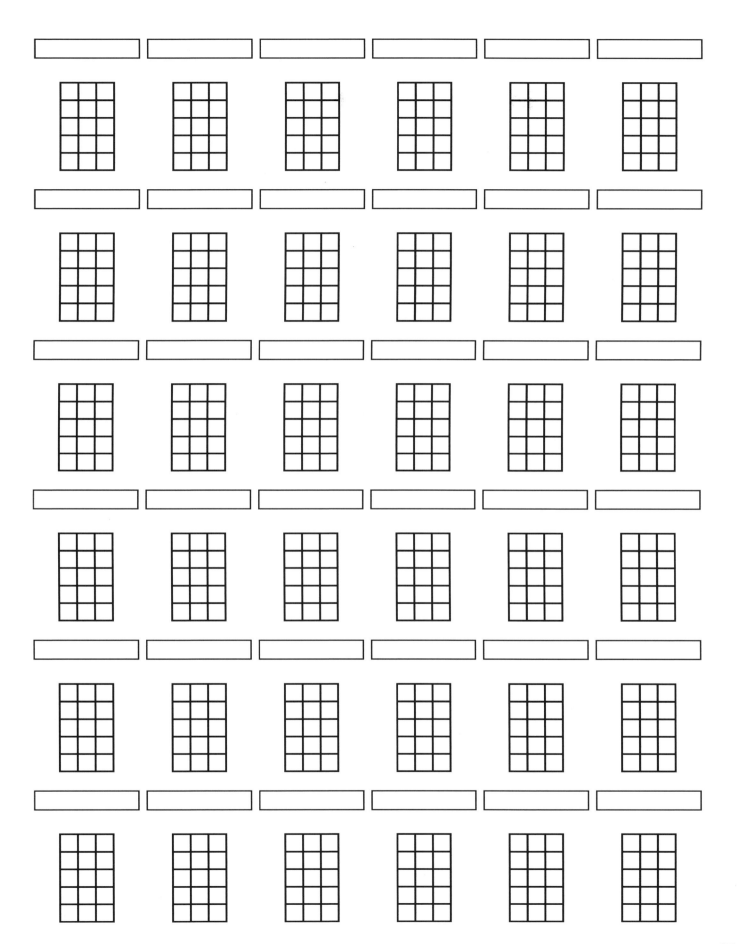

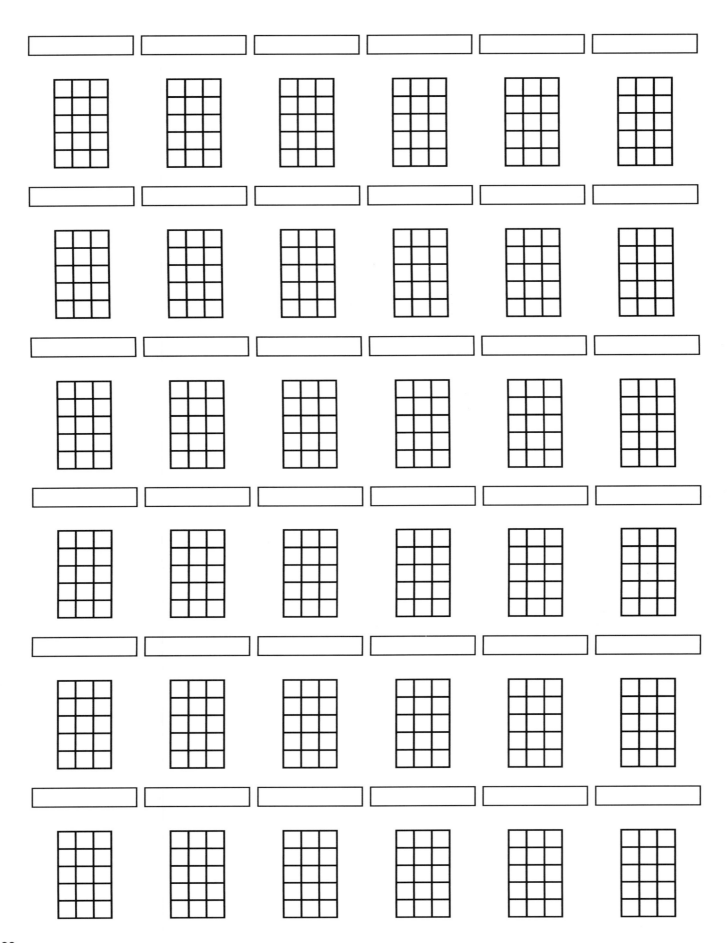

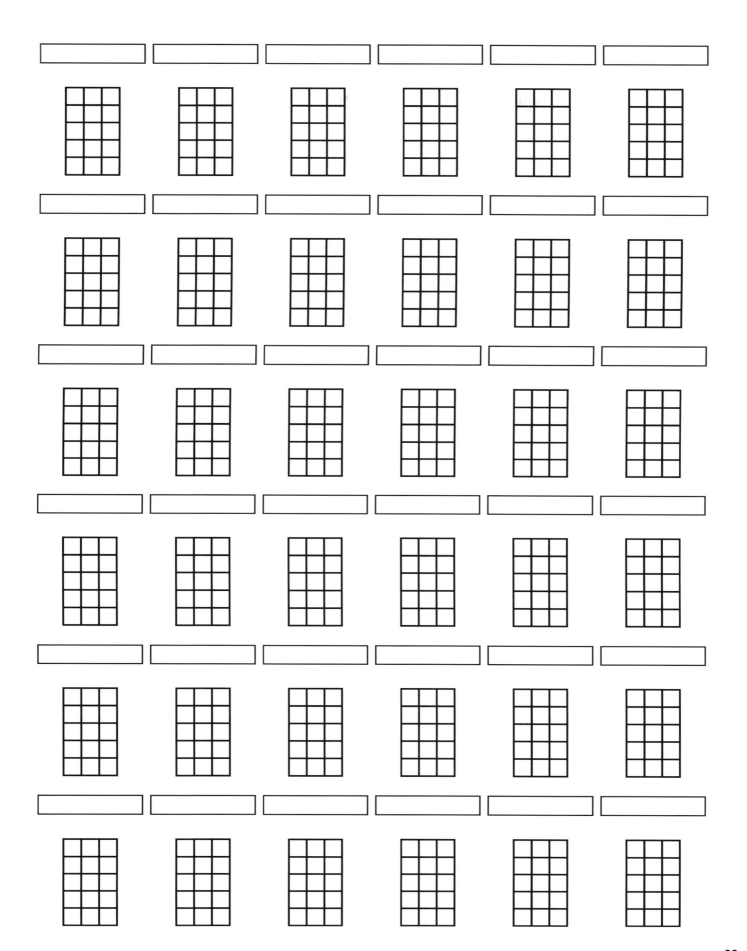

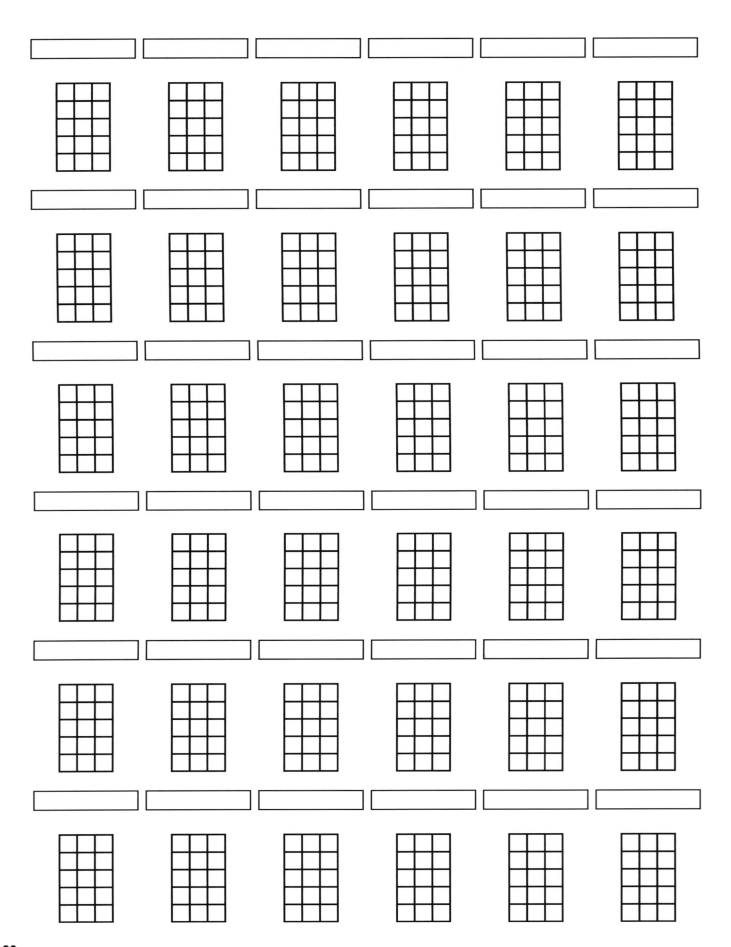

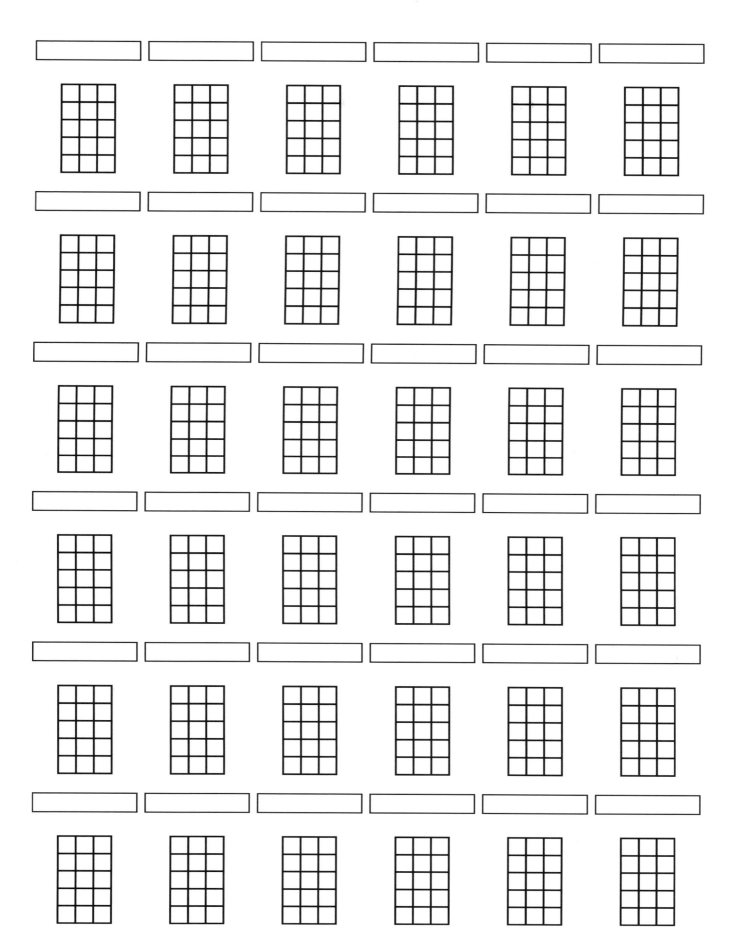

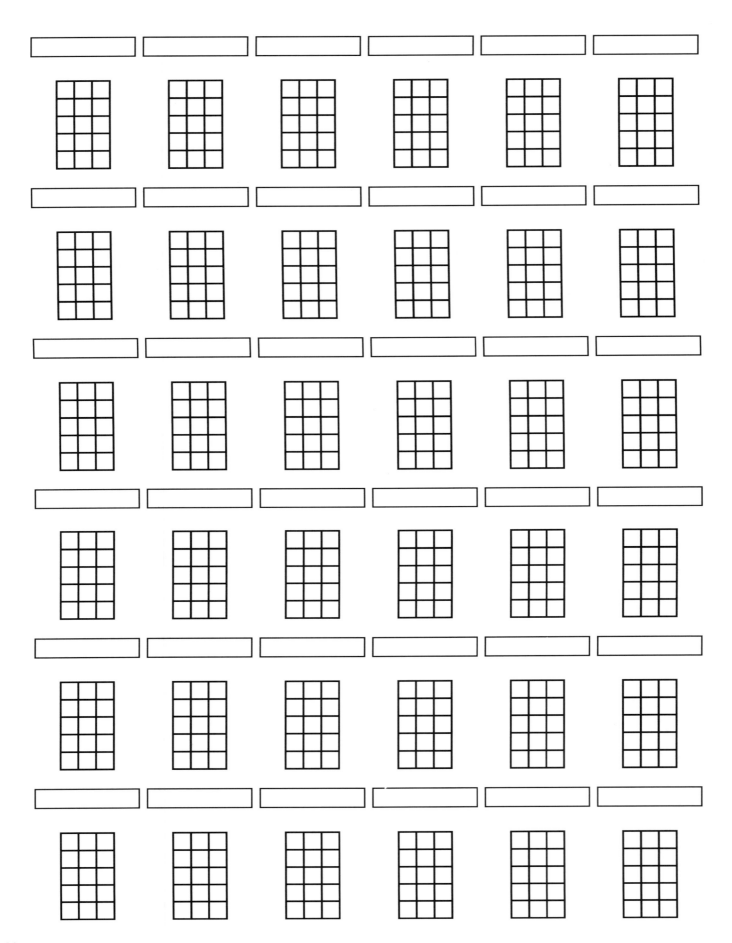

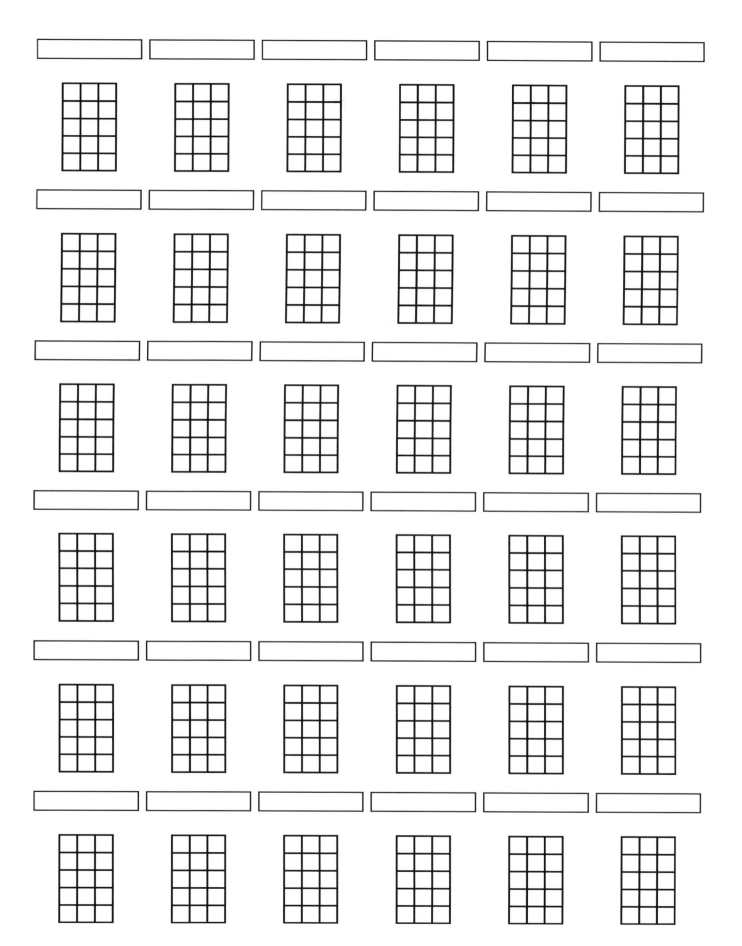

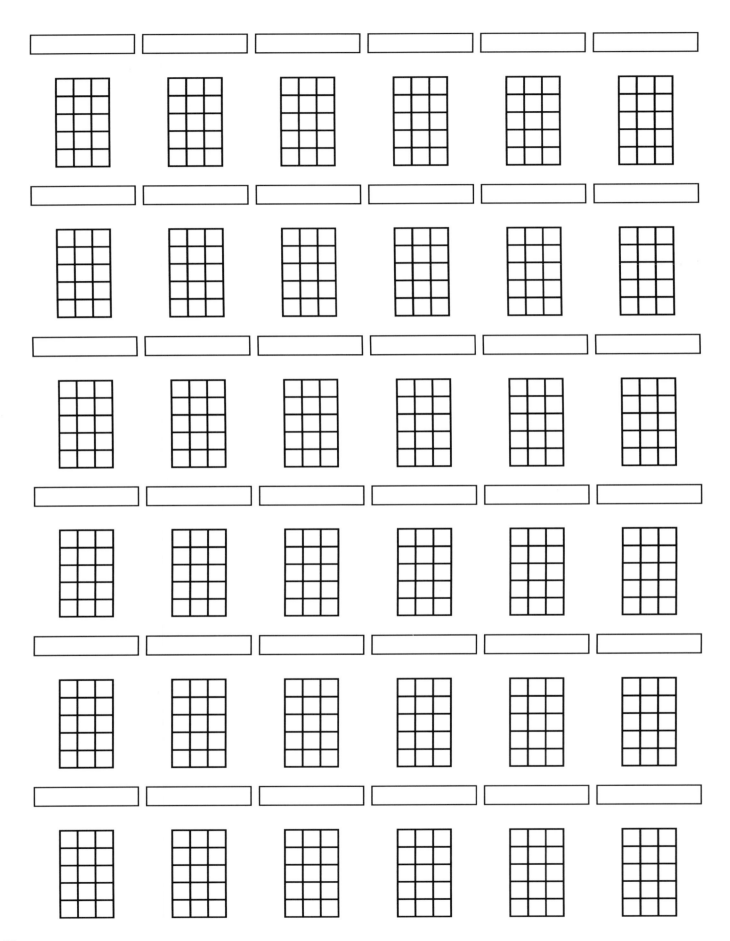

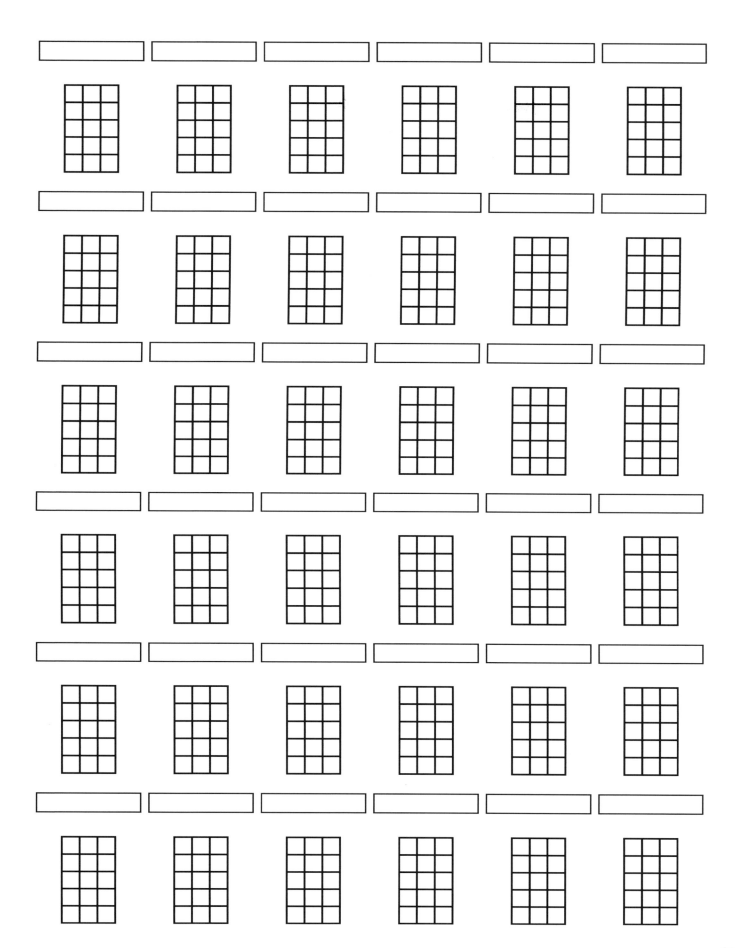

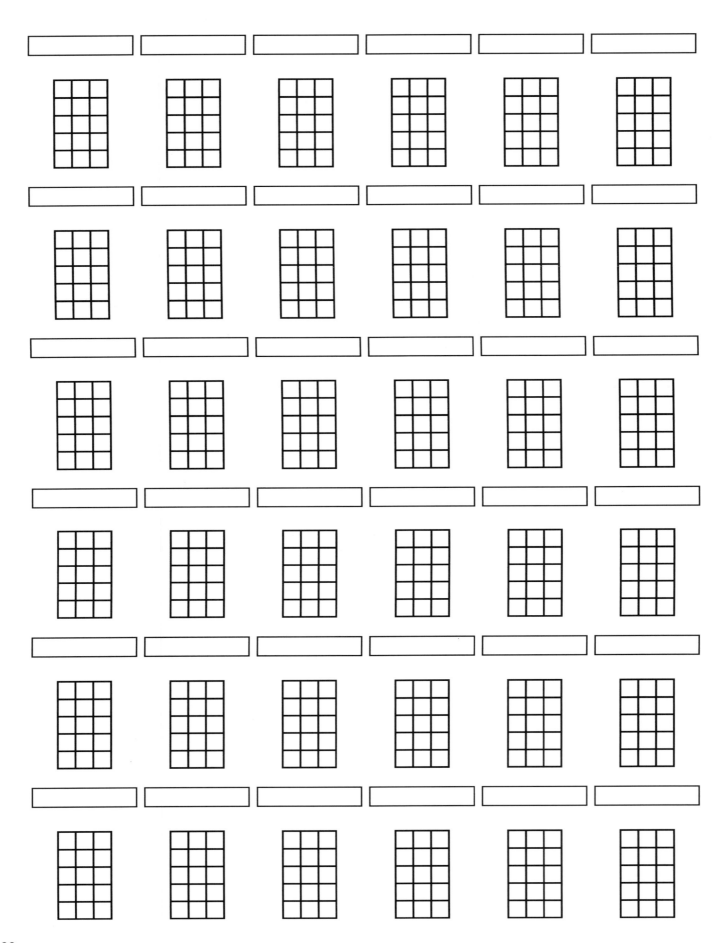

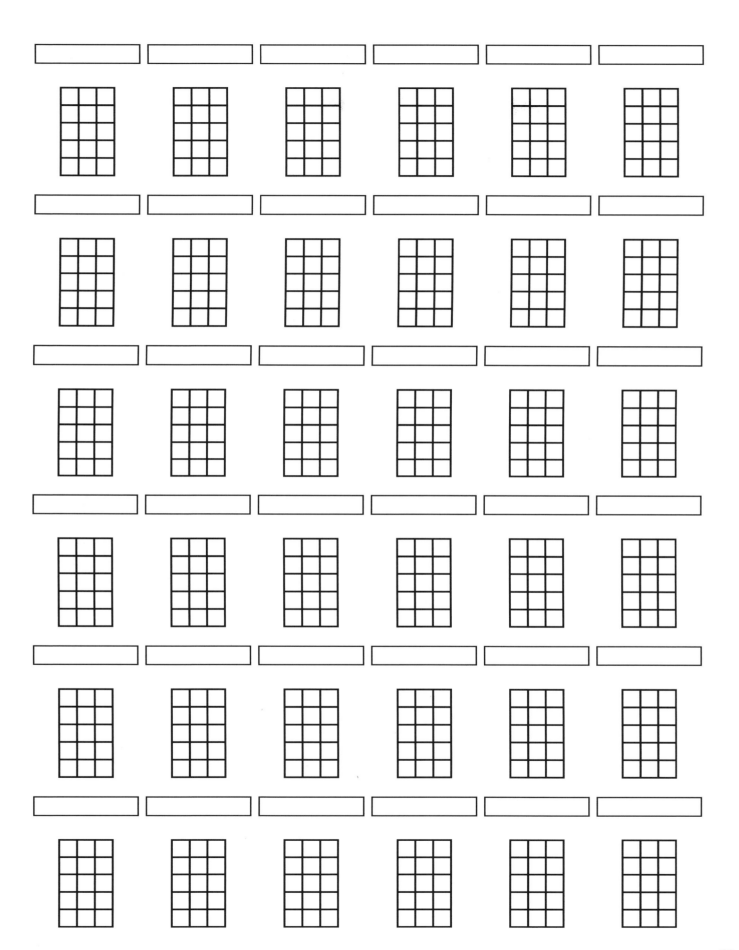

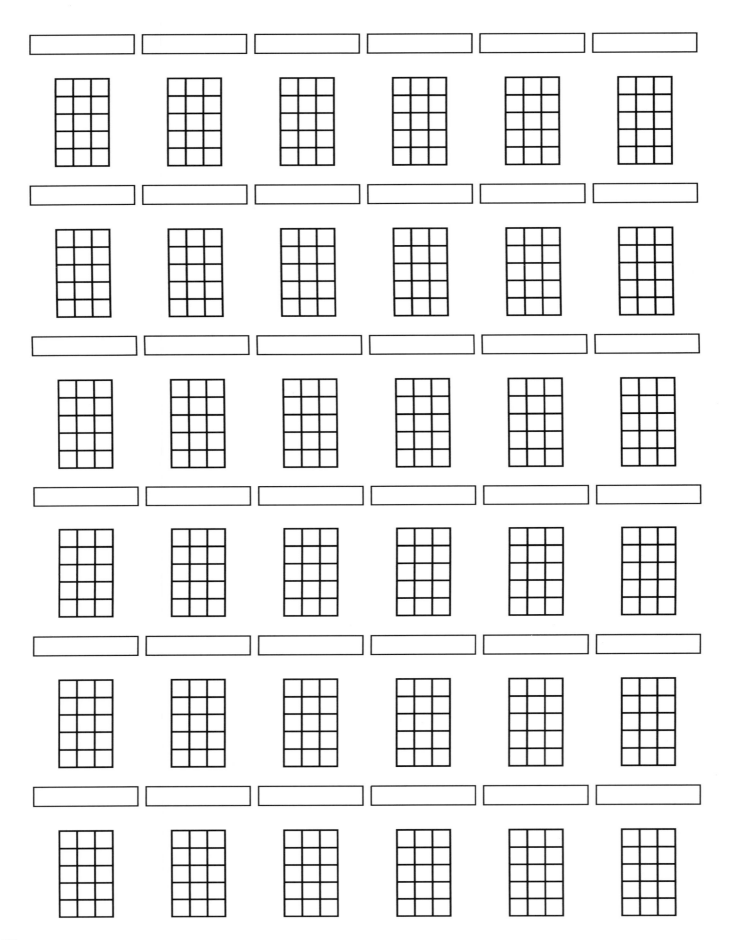

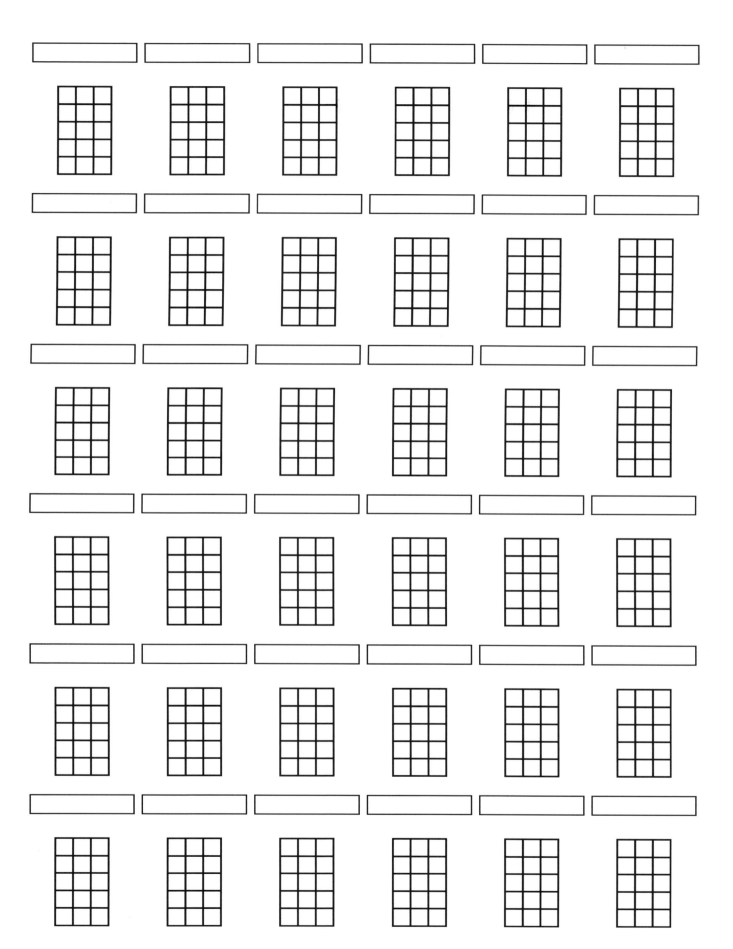

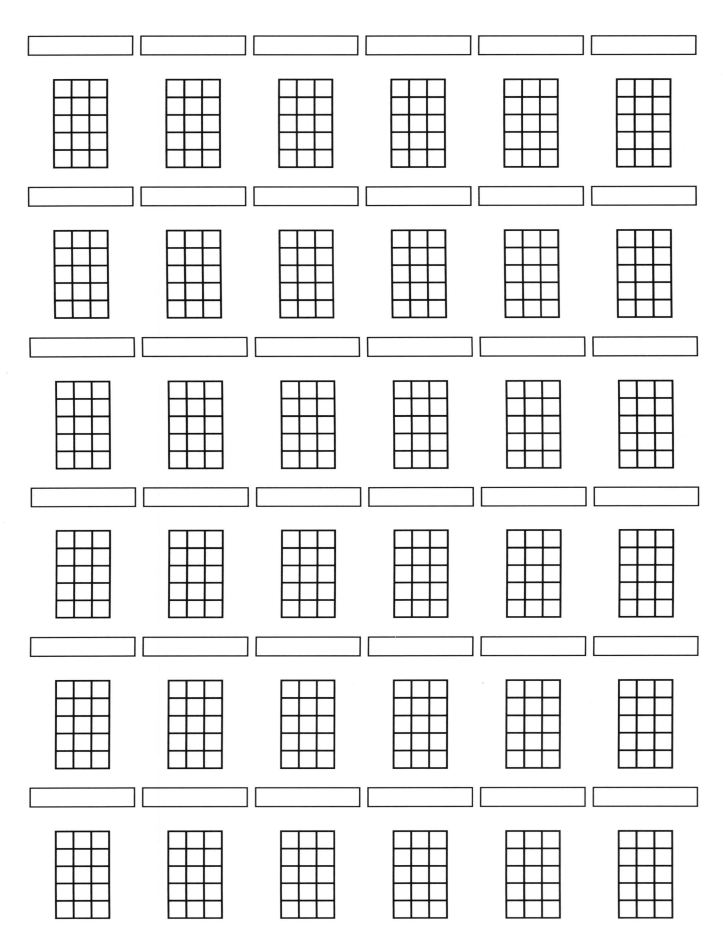

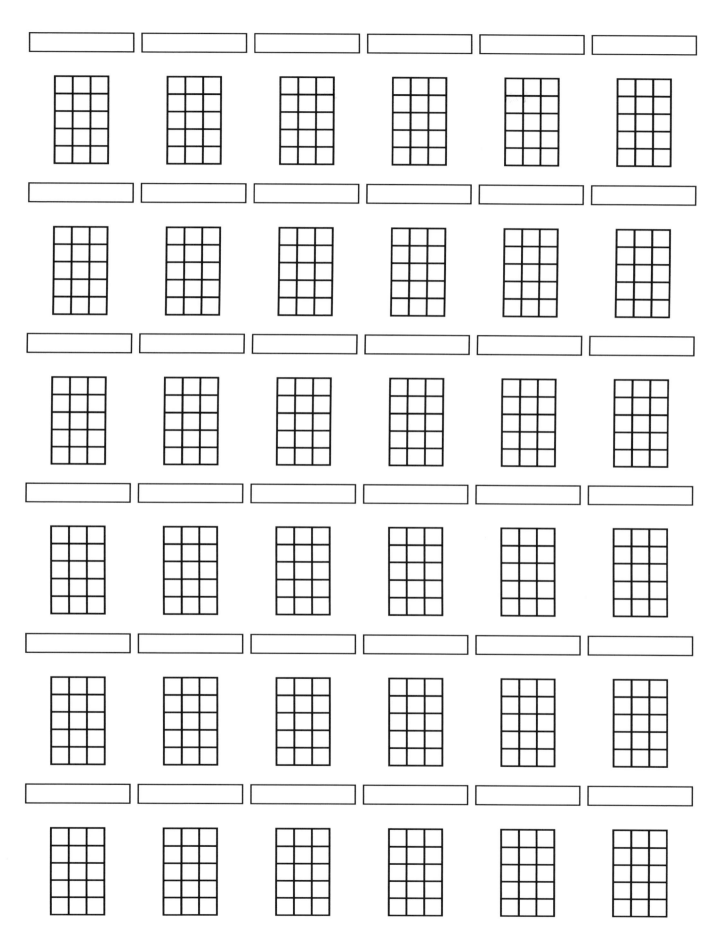

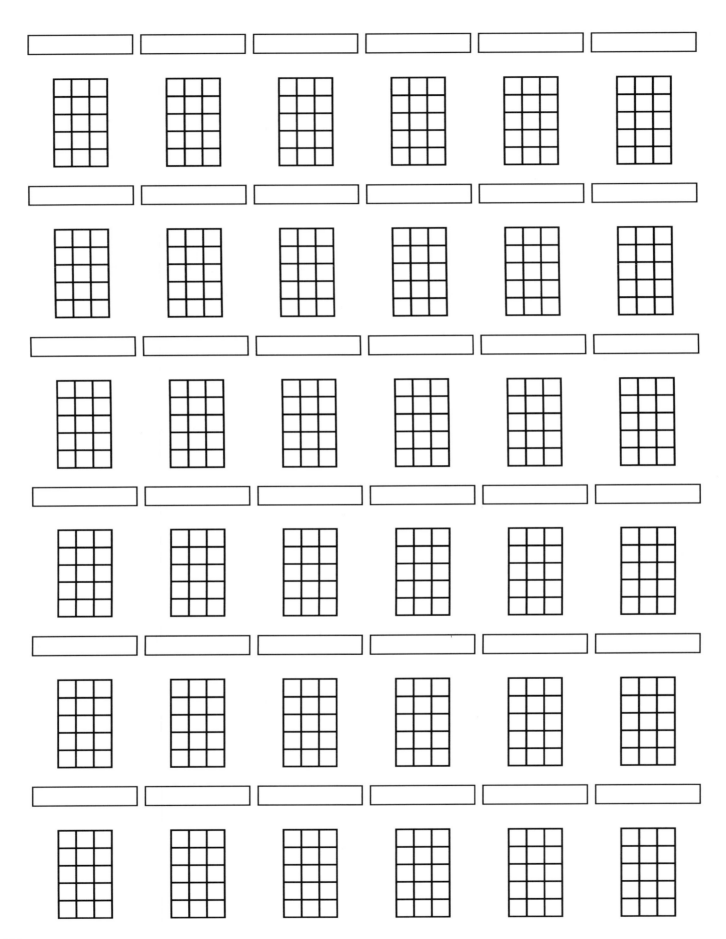

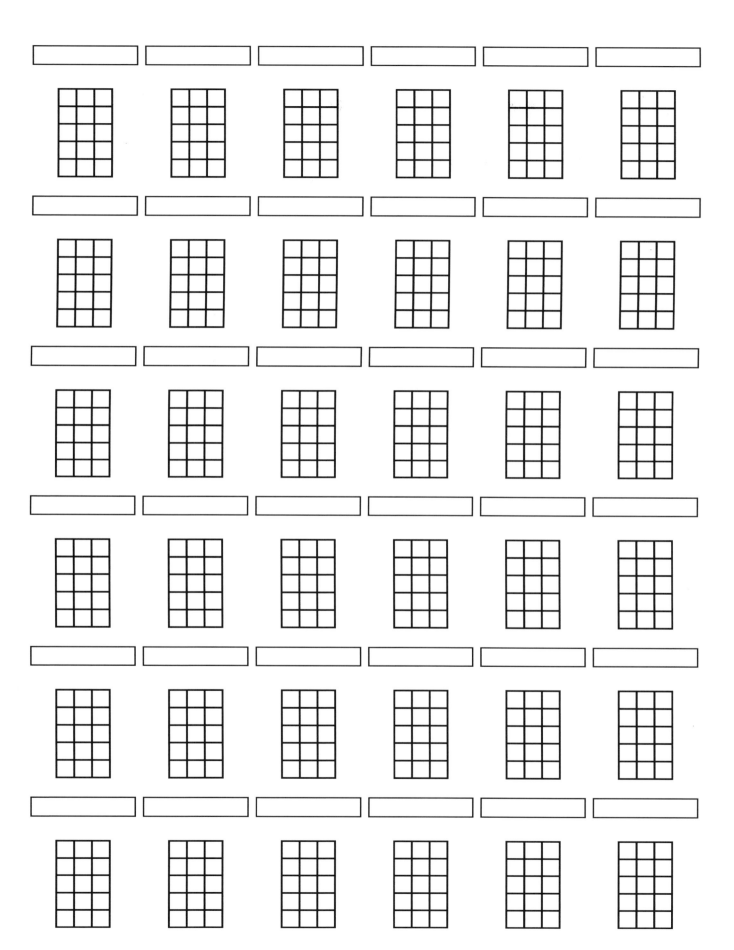

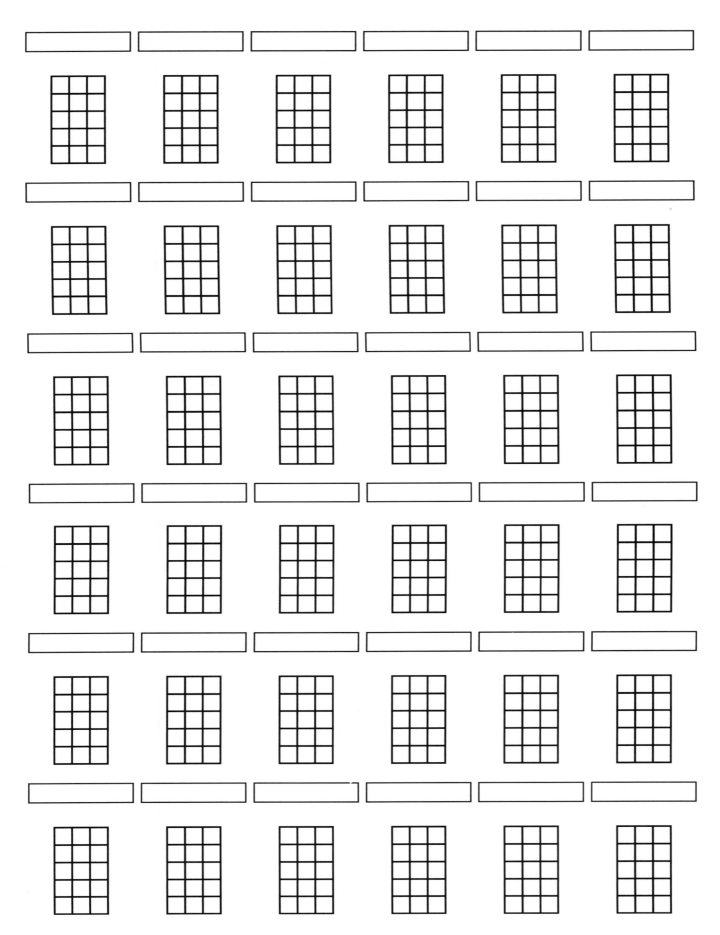

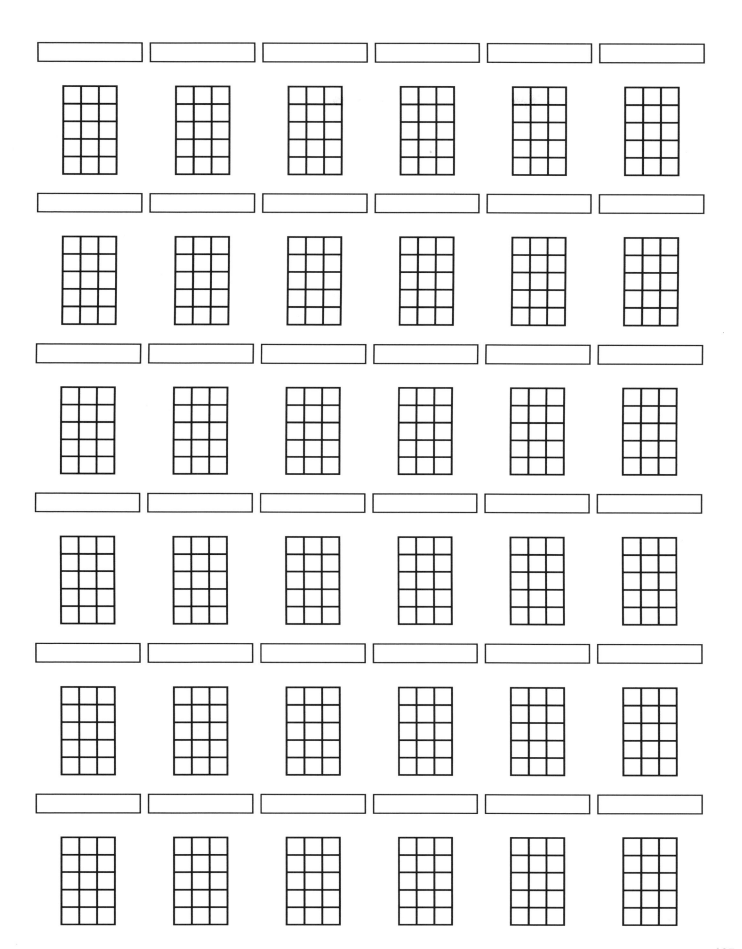

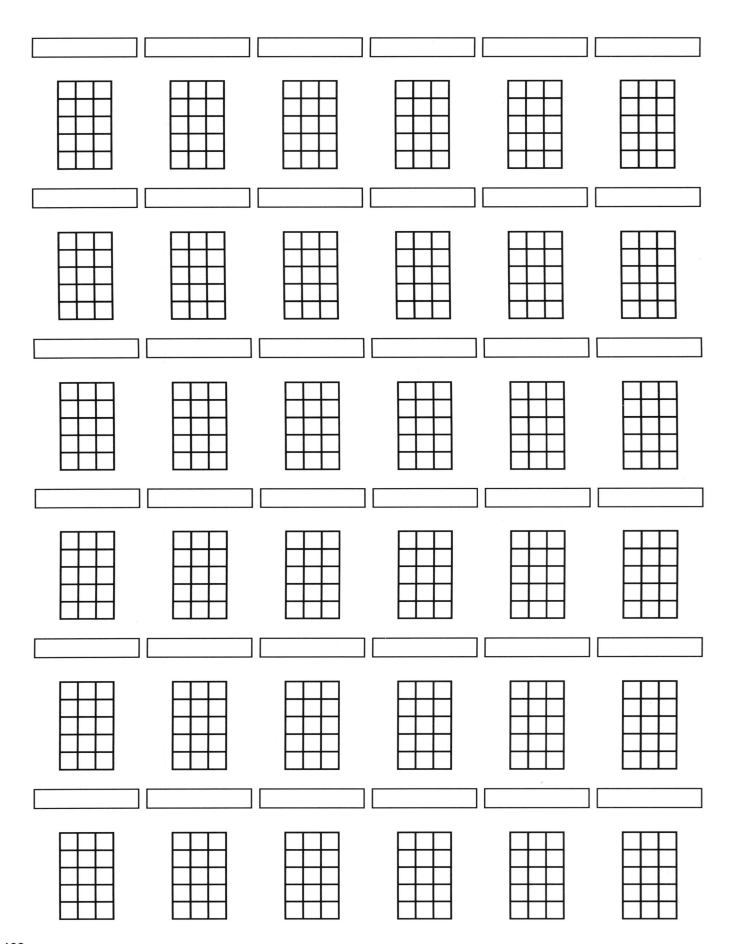

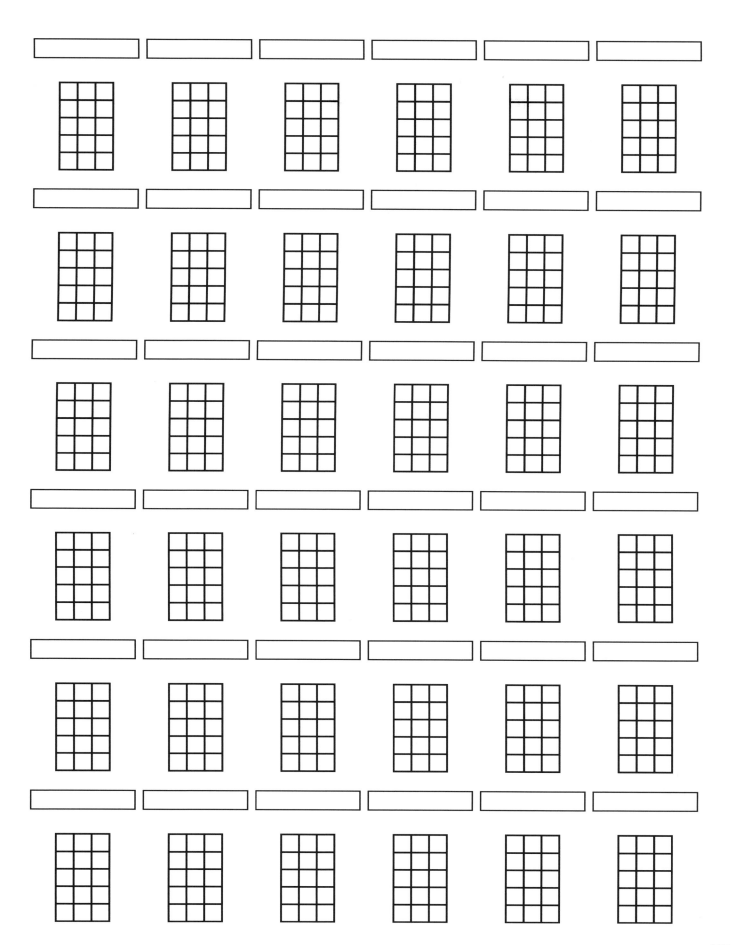

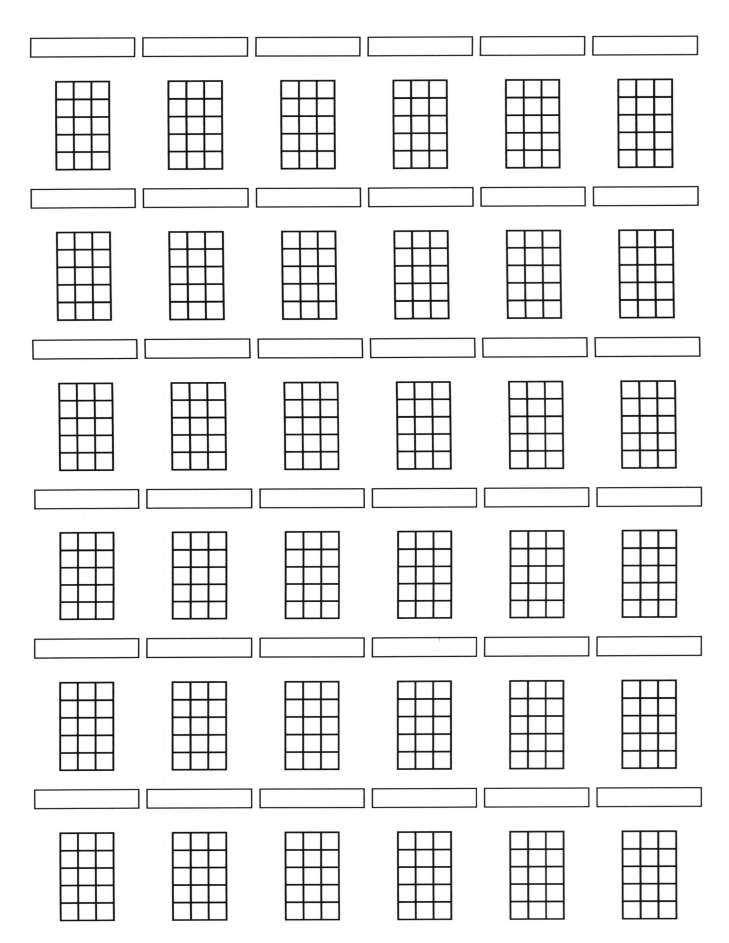

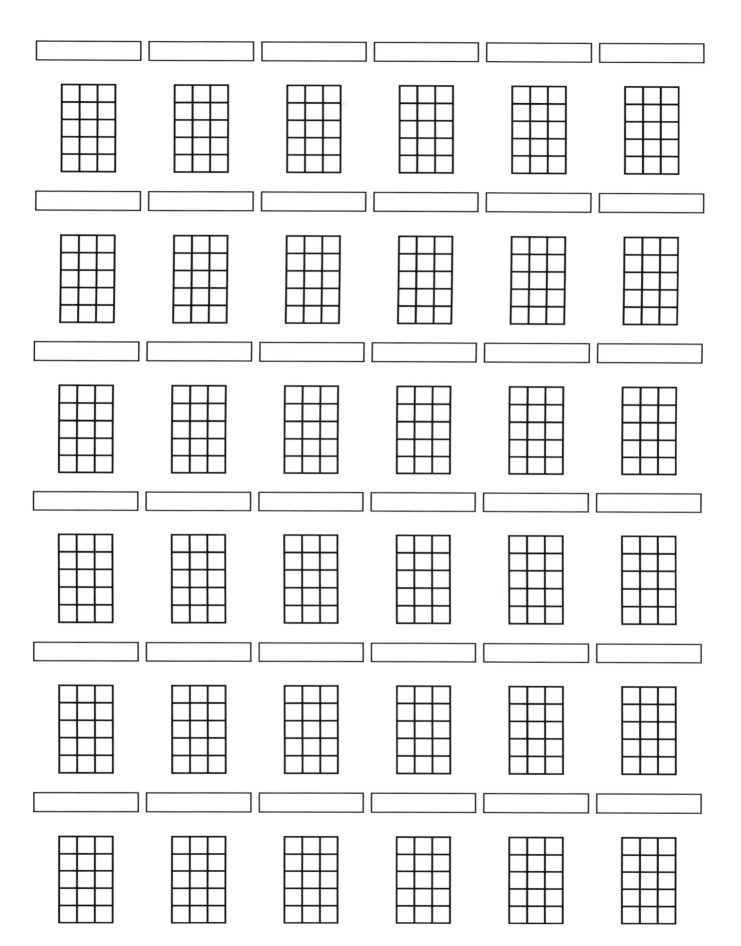

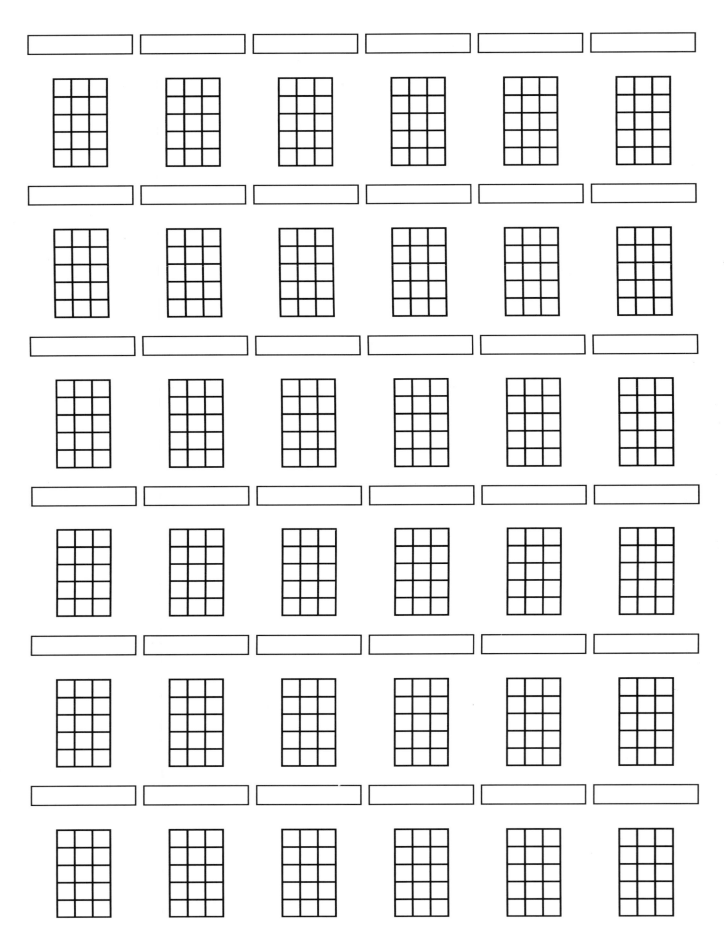

110